Wordsworth's Reading of Roman Prose

BY

JANE WORTHINGTON

ARCHON BOOKS
1970

Copyright, 1946, by Yale University Press
Reprinted 1970 with permission of Yale University Press
in an unaltered and unabridged edition

[*Yale Studies in English, Vol. 102*]

SBN: 208 00920 5
Library of Congress Catalog Card Number: 74-91194
Printed in the United States of America

PR
5892
.L5
W6
1970

To

MY MOTHER AND FATHER

PREFACE

THE title of this book is not entirely satisfactory. Its pedantic flavor causes me no regret, but I am discomforted to find that, correct as the title is, it often conjures up a false notion of what is to come. Until Wordsworth is recognized as a poet well read in ancient and modern literatures, such a title as *Wordsworth's Reading of Roman Prose* must continue to suggest an examination of minutiae. Perhaps this book will help to counteract misconceptions that, begun in his lifetime, even now persist. My thesis is not merely that Wordsworth read some Roman prose, but that he read widely, sometimes even intensively, and that his reading had an appreciable effect upon his thought and work.

The extent of his reading in Roman history and Roman political writing requires a chapter in itself. In that first chapter I also consider the stimulus given to Wordsworth's Roman studies by his association with the French revolutionists at a time when the ideals of republican Rome were being most actively cultivated. The second chapter is an attempt to estimate the effect of Roman political theory upon Wordsworth's own thought and work. The third, and last, chapter is a study of Wordsworth's reading in Roman Stoicism; here I present evidence which shows Wordsworth to have been profoundly influenced by the Roman Stoics, their influence being revealed in some of his finest poetry.

In its original form *Wordsworth's Reading of Roman Prose* was submitted as a dissertation to Yale University in candidacy for the degree of Doctor of Philosophy. The subject was suggested to me by Professor Frederick A. Pottle, under whose direction I have worked. For his good aid and counsel I am deeply grateful. I wish also to thank Professors Chauncey Brewster Tinker, Alfred R. Bellinger, and William K. Wimsatt, Jr., who read the dissertation and gave me valuable suggestions. From Dr. Cora Lutz and Dr. Norma Rose I have received assistance of various kinds. I appreciate also the help of Professor Benjamin Nangle, who read the final copy and gave me numerous suggestions.

Harvard University Library has kindly permitted me to use two Wordsworth manuscripts. To Dr. J. R. MacGillivray I am indebted for permission to use his unpublished Harvard dissertation. Professor Leslie N. Broughton has allowed me to examine Wordsworth's copy of Cato and other authors, now in the Wordsworth Collection at Cornell University Library; I am grateful for the many kindnesses he has shown me.

Connecticut College, 1945.

BIBLIOGRAPHICAL NOTE

THE *Poetical Works of Wordsworth*, edited by Thomas Hutchinson (London, Oxford University Press, 1932) has been used as the standard text for all references to Wordsworth's poetry with the exception of *The Prelude*. References to *The Prelude* are to the edition edited by Ernest De Selincourt (London, Oxford University Press, 1932).

The problem of selecting editions and translations for the classical authors has been a difficult one. With the Latin authors it has often been impossible to discover either the editions or the translations used by Wordsworth. But the indications are that Wordsworth read most of the Latin authors in the original. (See below, pp. 13-16.) Latin editions, therefore, have been used in this study. I have selected editions from the Loeb Classical Library and from the Bibliotheca Scriptorum Graecorum et Romanorum Teubneriana. (In my quotations from the Teubner texts I have normalized the use of capital letters.)

With the Greek authors I have found in important instances the translations used by Wordsworth (Plutarch; Polybius; Epictetus, *Manual;* Diogenes Laertius). I have also shown that Wordsworth read Greek prose only in translation. (See below, pp. 13-16.) Wherever possible I have used the translations used by Wordsworth. Where these are unknown, I have selected translations which were most popular and most readily acquired during Wordsworth's lifetime.

Cue Titles

CICERO, *Acad*	Marcus Tullius Cicero. *Academica.* H. Rackham, ed. and tr. Loeb Classical Library, 1933.
CICERO, *De Finibus*	—. *De Finibus Bonorum et Malorum.* H. Rackham, ed. and tr. Loeb Classical Library, 1914.
CICERO, *De Legibus*	—. *De Legibus.* C. W. Keyes, ed. and tr. Loeb Classical Library, 1928.
CICERO, *De Officiis*	—. *De Officiis.* W. Miller, ed. and tr. Loeb Classical Library, 1938.
CICERO, *Nat Deo*	—. *De Natura Deorum.* H. Rackham, ed. and tr. Loeb Classical Library, 1933.
CICERO, *Tusc Disp*	—. *Tusculan Disputations,* J. E. King, ed. and tr. Loeb Classical Library, 1927.
DIOGENES LAERTIUS	Diogenes Laërtius. *De Vitis, Dogmatis & Apophthegmatis Clarorum Philosophorum,* Libri X. [Henri Estienne, ed.] Cologne, 1616. Greek and Latin.

EL	*The Early Letters of William and Dorothy Wordsworth.* Ernest De Selincourt, ed. Oxford, 1935.
EPICTETUS, *Discourses*	"The Discourses of Epictetus," *All the Works of Epictetus.* Elizabeth Carter, tr. London, 1758.
EPICTETUS, *Manual*	Epictetus. *Manuale.* Joseph Simpson, ed. Oxford, 1739. Greek and Latin.
FLORUS	Lucius Annaeus Florus. E. S. Forster, ed. and tr. Loeb Classical Library, 1929.
HARPER	George McLean Harper. *William Wordsworth, His Life, Works, and Influence.* New York, 1916. 2 vols.
LIVY	Titus Livius. *Ab Urbe Condita.* M. Mueller, ed. Bibliotheca Teubneriana, 1926. 4 vols.
LY	*The Letters of William and Dorothy Wordsworth, The Later Years.* Ernest De Selincourt, ed. Oxford, 1939. 3 vols.
MARCUS AURELIUS, *Meditations*	Marcus Aurelius Antoninus. *His Meditations Concerning Himselfe.* Meric Casaubon, tr. London, 1634.
MY	*The Letters of William and Dorothy Wordsworth, The Middle Years.* Ernest De Selincourt, ed. Oxford, 1937. 2 vols.
NEPOS	Cornelius Nepos. J. C. Rolfe, ed. and tr. Loeb Classical Library, 1929.
PLUTARCH	*The Lives of the Noble Grecians and Romans,* Compared together, by that Grave Learned Philosopher and Historiographer, Plutarch of Chaeronea, Translated out of Greek into French, by James Amiot, And out of French into English, by Sir Thomas North. Cambridge, 1676.
POLYBIUS	*The History of Polybius the Megalopolitan.* Edward Grimeston, tr. London, 1634.
Prose Works	*The Prose Works of William Wordsworth.* Alexander B. Grosart, ed. London, 1876. 3 vols.
Rydal Mount	"The Rydal Mount Library Catalogue," reprinted in *Transactions of the Wordsworth Society,* No. 6, Edinburgh, pp. 195–257.
SALLUST, *Bell Cat*	Sallust. [The War with Catiline.] J. C. Rolfe, ed. and tr. Loeb Classical Library, 1931.

SALLUST, *Bell Jug*	Sallust. [The War with Jugurtha.] J. C. Rolfe, ed. and tr. Loeb Classical Library, 1931.
SENECA, *De Beneficiis*	L. Annaeus Seneca. *De Beneficiis.* C. Hosius, ed. Bibliotheca Teubneriana, 1914.
SENECA, *De Clementia*	—. *De Clementia.* C. Hosius, ed. Bibliotheca Teubneriana, 1914.
SENECA, *Dial*	—. *Dialogorum Libros XII.* E. Hermes, ed. Bibliotheca Teubneriana, 1923.
SENECA, *Ep*	—. *Ad Lucilium Epistulae Morales.* R. M. Gummere, ed. and tr. Loeb Classical Library, 1917–25. 3 vols.
SENECA, *NQ*	—. *Naturalium Quaestionum Libros VIII.* A. Gercke, ed. Bibliotheca Teubneriana, 1907.
TACITUS, *Agr*	Publius Cornelius Tacitus. *Agricola.* M. Hutton, ed. and tr. Loeb Classical Library, 1932.
TACITUS, *Ann*	—. *The Annals.* J. Jackson, ed. and tr. Loeb Classical Library, 1925–37. 4 vols.
TACITUS, *Hist*	—. *The Histories.* C. H. Moore, ed. and tr. Loeb Classical Library, 1925–37. 4 vols.

CONTENTS

Preface   vii

Bibliographical Note   ix

I. Wordsworth's Reading of Roman Historical and Political Writing   1

II. Roman Influence on Wordsworth's Political Thought   19

III. Wordsworth and Roman Stoicism   43

Appendix   75

Index   79

Wordsworth's Reading of Roman Prose

I

Wordsworth's Reading of Roman Historical
and
Political Writing

DURING his long and active career as a poet, William Wordsworth found time to acquire an extensive knowledge of Roman historical and political writing. It is the purpose of this chapter to show how this knowledge was acquired and to define with some precision its extent and nature.[1] To this end a chronological study offers the simplest and surest way.

In spite of the fullness of detail with which Wordsworth has described his years at school, information about his early reading—at least, in the classics—is remarkably limited. Except for a well-thumbed copy of the *Fables* of Phaedrus, I have found no evidence of his Latin studies at the Hawkshead School.[2] According to De Quincey, the school deserves little credit for Wordsworth's later skill in Latin;[3] in fact, De Quincey would have us believe that Wordsworth was "educated most negligently at Hawkshead."[4] In juvenile verses written for a school celebration, Wordsworth himself pays perfunctory respect to the classics and hastens on to extol "immortal Science."[5] (It is somewhat ironic that his praise of science should reveal a Lucretian enthusiasm for the "nature of things.") But, whatever the deficiencies tolerated at Hawkshead, the school must have given Wordsworth at least a respectable preparation in the classics. Certainly he ranked well among fellow students entering Cambridge in 1787.

---

1. K. Lienemann in his book, *Die Belesenheit von William Wordsworth* (Berlin, 1908), has collected all the reference notes to classic authors made by William Knight in his edition of *The Poetical Works of William Wordsworth* (Edinburgh, 1882–86, 8 vols.) and by Alexander B. Grosart in his edition of *The Prose Works of William Wordsworth* (London, 1876, 3 vols.). Dr. Lienemann has made no attempt to study the influence of Wordsworth's reading nor has he added anything new to Wordsworth scholarship. With the publication of De Selincourt's edition of the Wordsworth letters (1935–39), Dr. Lienemann's work became obsolete.
2. Wordsworth's copy of Phaedrus is now in the Swarthmore College Library.
3. *The Collected Writings of Thomas De Quincey*, David Masson, ed. (Edinburgh, 1889–90, 14 vols.), II, 265.
4. *Idem*, V, 204.
5. "Lines Written as a School Exercise at Hawkshead," *The Poetical Works of William Wordsworth*, E. De Selincourt, ed. (Oxford, 1940), pp. 259–61.

On October 30 of that year Wordsworth began his residence at St. John's College. The following week the *Admissions to the College* record that William Wordsworth was "admitted Foundress Scholar."[6] It was probably his advanced standing in mathematics rather than any special proficiency in the classics that brought him this honor.[7] Like all Cambridge colleges, St. John's had necessarily to respect mathematical ability, for university honors at that time depended almost wholly upon distinguished work in the sciences.[8] Nevertheless, St. John's was of all colleges the one most prominent for its instruction in the classics.

At the end of the eighteenth century the classical training of university students was mainly the responsibility of the individual colleges.[9] Evidence that St. John's faithfully attempted to fulfill its responsibility is found in the regular examinations instituted there in 1765.[1] These examinations were the first to be established in any college and they were required of all classes. The men of St. John's soon recognized and rejoiced in the distinction which the examinations brought to their college, and to preserve this distinction they jealously opposed the extension of their plan to the university as a whole.[2] As a student of St. John's, therefore, Wordsworth was regularly examined in the classics.[3] In Latin history, selections from Cicero, Livy, and Tacitus were to be expected.[4] Polybius was included in the reading program of a student in 1796.[5] According to Dorothy Wordsworth, Wordsworth's own reading program was devoted mainly to languages—Italian, Latin, Greek, etc.[10]

Passages in *The Prelude* suggest that his early reading in the classics included a fair proportion of historical and political writing. In *The Prelude* Wordsworth described himself as a youth versed in ancient story, one "whose breast had heaved Under the weight of classic eloquence,"[11] and he plainly admitted that he had long preferred the histories of Greece and Rome to those of his own country.[12] Moreover, about 1805 when Wordsworth was writing *The Prelude* he

---

6. *Admissions to the College of St John the Evangelist in the University of Cambridge*, Part 4 (July, 1767–July, 1802), Sir Robert Forsyth Scott, ed. (Cambridge, 1931), pp. 571–2; see also p. 56.

7. For Wordsworth's advanced standing in mathematics, see his "Autobiographical Memoranda," in Christopher Wordsworth, *Memoirs of William Wordsworth* (London, 1851, 2 vols.), I, 14.

8. Christopher Wordsworth, *Scholae Academicae* (Cambridge, 1877), pp. 44–58.

9. *Idem*, p. 118. Not until 1822–24 did the university establish a classical tripos (*idem*, pp. 20, 116).

1. *Idem*, p. 352.   2. *Idem*, p. 353.

3. The examinations, although instituted in 1765, were still in force during Wordsworth's time (*idem*, p. 255).

4. *Idem*, pp. 118, 354–7.   5. *Idem*, p. 118.

10. *EL*, p. 51. See also Wordsworth, *Memoirs of William Wordsworth*, I, 14.

11. *Prelude*, VII, 540–4.   12. *Idem*, VIII, 617–22.

found his mature taste approving the books he had "valued most" in his youth.[9] It will soon be shown that in 1805 Wordsworth's mature taste approved particularly the historical writing of early Rome.

But this special branch of classic learning left comparatively few marks upon his earliest poetic productions. The explanation is obvious. The young man who was "stirred to ecstasy . . . By glittering verse" chose to adorn his own with bits of Horace and to practise his phrasing in translations of Vergil and Catullus.[1] Roman prose offered no apparent aid to the poet who knew himself a "dedicated Spirit" and yet knew not to what end that spirit had been dedicated. Before Livy could compete with Vergil something was needed to illuminate the history of Rome, something to make its ancient concerns a present heritage.

Revolutionary France supplied this need. During Wordsworth's residence in France he found the men whom he most respected reflecting in their life and thought the ideas of republican Rome. He could not help being impressed with the significance of classical history when he found modern concepts of antiquity directing the actions of men who had brought France to "the top of golden hours." Such a discovery worked a fundamental change in Wordsworth's attitude toward the prose writers of classic Rome.

Harold Talbot Parker is almost the only scholar who has considered the phenomenon of classical influence upon the French political leaders. Before examining at first hand those particulars of the phenomenon which concerned Wordsworth, we may reach a general appreciation of the whole by a brief summary of Dr. Parker's book, *The Cult of Antiquity and the French Revolutionaries*.[2]

Dr. Parker has examined the debates in the National Assembly, the Legislative Assembly, the National Convention, and also nine revolutionary newspapers. From such varied sources of French thought he has collected a wealth of material. He concludes that the classics which mattered to the revolutionists were essentially Roman in character.[3] As a general rule the revolutionists cited the authors they had read in their *collèges*, and these authors, with the single exception of Plutarch, were all Latin.[4] Cicero was most often cited, then Horace and Plutarch, Tacitus, Vergil, Seneca, Livy, and Sallust.[5]

9. *Idem*, VI, 99–100.
1. See *The Poetical Works of William Wordsworth*, E. De Selincourt, ed. (Oxford, 1940): "An Evening Walk," B-text, ll. 72–8 (see also Wordsworth's translation of Horace, *Odes*, III, 13, appended to the above passage); "The Death of a Starling—Catullus," p. 263; "Orpheus and Eurydice," p. 283; "The Horse," p. 285; "Ode to Apollo," p. 286.
2. Chicago, 1937. Reviewed by Carl Becker, *The Philosophical Review*, XLVI (July, 1937), 440–1; Geoffrey Bruun, *Classical Weekly*, XXX (May 17–24, 1937), 286–7.
3. Parker, *op. cit.*, p. 17.   4. *Idem*, pp. 14–21.   5. *Idem*, pp. 18–19.

But, aside from these conclusions on the general nature of the cult, Dr. Parker also analyzes its shifting fortunes during the years 1789 to 1795. When the revolutionary movement was first getting under way the references to antiquity were taken quite seriously. People believed that history could teach them solutions to their problems in the light of the success or failure with which the ancients had handled similar problems. As a rule, the Center and Left urged men to follow the examples of the early Romans, while the Right warned men to avoid such examples.[6] That some leaders condemned and others praised the early Republic makes no difference to Dr. Parker's thesis. The general attitude was a serious one and both sides believed that Roman history offered an important lesson.

In the period that succeeded, debates centering upon antiquity became fewer. From October, 1791, to August, 1792, the Legislative Assembly was concerned with specific problems of the moment rather than with large, general issues. To a discussion of the legislation then being debated, classical literature contributed no more than an occasional tag.[7] But, when the National Convention opened in September, 1792, another decisive turn was given to the French dependence upon the classics. It was felt that the Republic of France could survive only by undergoing a kind of moral regeneration which would ultimately produce characters similar to those found in Plutarch or Livy.[8] For the sake of the Republic, Frenchmen should practise *public virtue* in the Spartan sense of devotion to country and *private virtue* in the Roman sense of personal austerity. Now men returned to the *philosophe* discussions of Montesquieu and Rousseau, eager to learn their interpretations of Roman legislation.[9] It was not long before the new impulse began to express itself in the outward symbols of pure fad; eventually—Camillus Gracchus Babeuf in a Phrygian cap.[1]

It was in such a "climate of opinion" that Wordsworth became a resident of France. He arrived at Dieppe, November 27, 1791; he was in Paris, November 30 to December 5, at which time he attended the National Assembly; and he reached Orleans on December 6.[2] He spent at least the early spring and summer of 1792 in Blois, but he returned to Orleans the first part of September.[3] He was again in

6. *Idem*, p. 84. See also pp. 94–5.   7. *Idem*, pp. 116–18.
8. *Idem*, pp. 119–38.   9. *Idem*, pp. 121–2.
1. *Idem*, pp. 139–45.
2. See *EL*, pp. 60, 66, and J. R. MacGillivray, *Times Literary Supplement*, April 24, 1930.
3. The fact that Wordsworth was in Blois by early spring is deduced from his letter of May 17, 1792 (see *EL*, p. 74). He was still in Blois, September 3 (see *EL*, p. 77), but according to his "Autobiographical Memoranda" he was in Orleans at the time of the September massacres (Wordsworth, *Memoirs of William Wordsworth*, I, 15).

Paris probably as early as the first week in October, and he remained there until the end of December, 1792.[4]

Let us relate these dates to the changing periods of classical influence marked out by Dr. Parker. Wordsworth entered France after the first excited discussions on antiquity had somewhat subsided. He could not know the sudden awakening felt by the early republicans when they left the world of Plutarch they had known in their *collèges* and entered the Paris of Louis XVI.[5] In the early winter of 1791 when Wordsworth attended the National Assembly he was probably unaware of any pronounced classical atmosphere. If he noticed at all the rhetorical references to antiquity he might have thought of them as nothing more than the mannerisms of a strange parliament.

Before Wordsworth entered upon the more active, dramatic scenes of the National Convention when the classical references again became pertinent and extended, he was allowed a period of initiation. At Orleans and later at Blois he learned something of the new philosophical history which since the middle of the century had characterized the intellectual thought of France.[6] Such an introduction was necessary for one who

> . . . was unprepared
> With needful knowledge, had abruptly passed
> Into a theatre, whose stage was filled
> And busy with an action far advanced.[7]

De Selincourt has assumed that the September massacres to which Wordsworth referred were those that occurred in Paris; he, therefore, dates Wordsworth's return to Orleans September 4 or 5 (*Prelude*, p. 567). J. R. MacGillivray, on the other hand, thinks that Wordsworth's return visit should be dated by the massacres which occurred in Orleans, September 15 ("Wordsworth and His Revolutionary Acquaintances, 1791–1797" [Ph.D. dissertation, Harvard University, 1930], pp. 67–9). But Eugène Bimbenet (*Histoire de la ville d'Orléans* [Orléans, 1884–88, 5 vols.], v, 1213) dates the Orleans' massacres September 16 and 17. I am inclined to accept De Selincourt's date, for Wordsworth in writing his "Memoranda" in 1847 would probably have had in mind the greater and more important massacres of Paris; also Wordsworth's other references were clearly to national rather than local events.

4. See below, p. 8.

5. See, for example, C. Desmoulins, "Histoire des Brissotins," *Archives Parlementaires de 1787 à 1860*, Première Série (1787 à 1799), (Paris, 1867–1913, 82 vols.), LXXV (Oct. 3, 1793), 622, n. 1: Speaking of the republicans of 1789, Desmoulins says: "Ces républicains étaient la plupart des jeunes gens qui, nourris de la lecture de Cicéron dans les collèges, s'y étaient passionnés pour la liberté. On nous élevait dans les écoles de Rome et d'Athènes, et dans la fierté de la République, pour vivre dans l'abjection de la monarchie, et sous le règne des Claude et des Vitellius. Gouvernement insensé qui croyait que nous pouvions nous enthousiasmer pour les pères de la patrie, du capitole, sans prendre en horreur les mangeurs d'hommes, de Versailles, et admirer le passé sans condamner le présent, *ulteriora mirari, praesentia secuturos.*"

6. For an analysis of the "new history," see Carl L. Becker, *The Heavenly City of the Eighteenth-Century Philosophers* (New Haven, 1932), pp. 71–118.

7. *Prelude*, IX, 92–5.

At Blois Wordsworth's schooling in republicanism fell under the skilled tutelage of Michel Beaupuy. In *The Prelude* Wordsworth nostalgically describes the sweetness of the academic groves where he wandered in philosophic talk with the noble Beaupuy. The description significantly draws upon Plutarch for the telling comparison.

> Such conversation, under Attic shades,
> Did Dion hold with Plato; ripened thus
> For a Deliverer's glorious task,—and such
> He, on that ministry already bound,
> Held with Eudemus and Timonides,
> Surrounded by adventurers in arms,
> When those two vessels with their daring freight,
> For the Sicilian Tyrant's overthrow,
> Sailed from Zacynthus,—philosophic war,
> Led by Philosophers.[8]

Wordsworth's admiration was apparently well founded, for the nobility of the Frenchman shines brightly even through the pages of modern scholarly biography.[9] He was a philosopher who devoted his life to a selfless cause. His calm, unwavering devotion to the good of society was based upon a philosophical faith in the power of ordinary men to make this life on earth a better one. In this faith, therefore, he was closely allied to the famous philosophers of the eighteenth century.[1] In his talks with Wordsworth the spirit of Montesquieu everywhere presided.[2]

It is well known that the eighteenth-century philosophers exploited ancient history for all it was worth. Montesquieu and Rousseau are two "philosophers" sufficiently opposed to one another and sufficiently important to Wordsworth to be mentioned as representative. In his *Considérations sur les causes de la grandeur des Romains et de leur décadence* and in his *De l'Esprit des lois*, Montesquieu over and over again deduces principles of government from the experience of the Romans.[3] Rousseau, though less obviously the historian, also draws support for his political arguments from the history of Rome.[4]

---

8. *Idem*, IX, 408–17.
9. See Georges Bussière and Émile Legouis, *Le Général Michel Beaupuy* (Paris, 1891).
1. For the articles of faith of the philosophers, see Becker, *op. cit.*, pp. 102–03.
2. Émile Legouis, *The Early Life of William Wordsworth*, J. W. Matthews, tr. (London, 1932), p. 207.
3. For a complete analysis of Montesquieu's use of antiquity in *Esprit des Lois*, see Lawrence Meyer Levin, *The Political Doctrine of Montesquieu's Esprit des Lois: Its Classical Background* (New York, 1936). For the influence of his "Historical Method" in England, see F. T. H. Fletcher, *Montesquieu and English Politics* (London, 1939), pp. 71–9.
4. See J. J. Rousseau, *Œuvres complètes* (Paris, 1871–77), III, 298 ("De l'Économie politique"); III, 310–11, 328 ("Du Contrat social").

One of his principles which later became important in Wordsworth's political thought is based upon the close connection that he found existing between the republican institutions of Rome and the "republican" virtues of its people.[5]

Under the direction of such philosophers Beaupuy initiated Wordsworth's training in republicanism. They talked history, "summoned up the honourable deeds Of ancient Story," thought "How quickly mighty Nations have been formed, From least beginnings." And in true Rousseau fashion they discovered in France's *political* revolution evidence of *moral* regeneration.

> . . . Elate we looked
> Upon their virtues; saw, in rudest men,
> Self-sacrifice the firmest; generous love,
> And continence of mind, and sense of right,
> Uppermost in the midst of fiercest strife.[6]

According to Professor Harper, Beaupuy took an active part in a political club at Blois, known as "La Société des Amis de la Constitution."[7] It is very likely that through some such society Wordsworth became familiar not only with the ideas of the leading revolutionists of the day but also with the men themselves. Eventually he chose to ally himself with the Brissotins, who at that time were the leading members of the Girondist party.[8] Tradition has it that on Wordsworth's return visit to Paris he lodged in the same house with Brissot.[9]

The Girondists as a whole are generally recognized as the most classically minded of all revolutionists, and Wordsworth's interest in antiquity has been laid to their account.[1] But curiously enough Brissot himself disparaged the cult of antiquity. Before 1789 Brissot had admired the ancient republics, but by 1792 he had come to believe them unsuitable as models for the large modern country of France.[2] In his political thought America had quite displaced the ancients. From Brissot's writings, therefore, Wordsworth was un-

---

5. Rousseau, *op. cit.*, I, 6, 8–9 ("Si le rétablissement des sciences et des arts a contribué à épurer les moeurs"); III, 290–1 ("De l'Économie politique"); III, 330, 335 ("Du Contrat social").

6. *Prelude*, IX, 385–9.   7. Harper, I, 152–5, 168.

8. Wordsworth, *Memoirs of William Wordsworth*, I, 76–7: "If he had remained longer in the French capital, he would, in all probability, have fallen a victim among the Brissotins, with whom he was intimately connected."

9. MacGillivray, "Wordsworth and His Revolutionary Acquaintances, 1791–1797," pp. 21, 78.

1. De Selincourt, *Prelude*, p. 576; Raymond Dexter Havens, *The Mind of a Poet* (Baltimore, 1941), pp. 504, 555; MacGillivray, "Wordsworth and His Revolutionary Acquaintances, 1791–1797," p. 84.

2. Parker, *op. cit.*: for Brissot's admiration of the Roman Republic, see pp. 37–8, 49–52; 60–1; for his revised opinion, see pp. 66–8, 101, 107–08.

likely to look fondly upon the past. But on the other hand the French Cicero had been too well trained in the classics completely to divorce himself from the Romans. He went to them for the sake of rhetoric, to support his attacks upon the Catilines of Paris, and to study various forms of political behavior.[3]

Wordsworth's period of initiation, which we have just described, can be briefly summed up. At Blois he became familiar with the *philosophe* theories of history; he talked ancient history with Beaupuy; and as a Girondist he was accustomed to political discussions heavily marked with classical references. In a word—he was prepared for the debates of the National Convention.

The dates of Wordsworth's return visit to Paris are unfortunately obscure. He was at Orleans during the September massacres,[4] and in Paris he speaks of the massacres' being divided from him by "one little month."[5] Dorothy Wordsworth's first mention of his return to England is December 22.[6] We can, therefore, calculate that at the most Wordsworth was in Paris from the first week in October until late in December.

The months of October, November, and December, 1792, present some of the most exciting of all chapters in the history of the Revolution. And what matters to us is that they are written in the language of the neo-Romans. In the summary made of Dr. Parker's book it has already been pointed out that the desire to accomplish a moral regeneration provided a new impetus to things Roman. An examination of the *Archives Parlementaires* for the closing months of 1792 and of two Girondist papers (one edited by Carra and another by Gorsas, journalists mentioned particularly by Wordsworth)[7] has convinced me of Dr. Parker's discriminating restraint. The close relationship between republicanism and virtue, which Rousseau had stressed and illustrated out of Roman history, was frequently expounded.[8] The heroic figures of Rome were regularly set up as models of virtuous conduct.[9] French republicans were constantly urged to imitate Ro-

---

3. See, for example, J. P. Brissot, *À tous les républicains de France, sur la société des Jacobins de Paris* (À Paris, Réimprimé à Londres, 1794), p. 177; *À ses Commettans, sur la situation de la convention* . . . (À Paris, Réimprimé à Londres, 1794), pp. 18, 39, 43, 46–7, 83, 97, 135, 140, 149, 159, 162.

4. See above, p. 4, n. 3.

5. *Prelude*, x, 74. Havens, *op. cit.*, p. 518, argues convincingly that Wordsworth returned to Paris earlier than De Selincourt has suggested.

6. *EL*, p. 82. De Selincourt, *Prelude*, p. 567, says that Wordsworth was in Paris "till the end of the year, or possibly till early in January 1793."

7. *Prelude*, IX, 176.

8. See *Le Courrier des départemens*, Ant.-Jos. Gorsas, éd., Vol. I, No. 10 (Oct. 1, 1792), pp. 159–60.

9. *Idem*, Vol. I, No. 1 (Sept. 22, 1792), p. 11; No. 2 (Sept. 23, 1792), pp. 24–5; No. 3 (Sept. 24, 1792), p. 45; No. 8 (Nov. 8, 1792), p. 114. *Annales patriotiques et littéraires*, M. Mercier et M. Carra, éds., No. 277 (Oct. 3, 1792), p. 1235.

man simplicity of manners; for example, they were persuaded to do away with all titled address for the simpler style of the Romans.[1]

But the Romans were called to the republican colors to direct also other kinds of programs. Their aid was invoked for all kinds of political action. The end of October saw debates and opinions on the decree forbidding members of the Convention to hold public office for six years following the ratification of the Constitution. These debates frequently turned upon the wisdom or stupidity of Lycurgus in exiling himself from Sparta after providing his people with a constitution.[2] Censure of the Jacobins or of the Paris Commune was the necessary and dangerous business of the Girondists; they successfully veiled the directness of attack by apt quotations from Sallust[3] or by judicious use of analogy to ancient violators of the state.[4]

In the long and heated arguments on the judgment of Louis it is not impossible for a modern reader actually to confuse the Bourbons and Tarquins or, less frequently, Louis and Caesar.[5] On December 16, 1792, Louvet presented the *ne plus ultra* in classical oratory. He spoke not at all as Louvet de Couvrai, but solely as Brutus; he translated into French the oration of Brutus to the Romans as it appeared in the second book of Livy's history.[6] Louvet developed at length the parallel between Philippe-Egalité and Collatinus, the liberal nephew of Tarquin the Proud. He apostrophized Philippe to impose upon himself a similar self-exile.[7]

Louvet has here been specifically named not only because among many eloquent Girondists he alone merited a prominent place in Wordsworth's *Prelude*,[8] but also because Wordsworth's interest in him was apparently a lasting one. His boldness in accusing Robespierre stood in effective contrast to the timidity of the indecisive good and won him the wholehearted admiration of the English poet.[9] Certainly it is safe to assume that Dorothy Wordsworth's read-

---

1. *Annales patriotiques et littéraires*, Supplément au No. 277 (Sept. 28, 1792), p. 1213: "Républicains comme les Romains, plus libres qu'eux, destinés à être vertueux, imitons leur exemple: ne faisons précéder les noms d'aucun titre: disons Pétion, Condorcet, Payne, comme on disoit à Rome Caton, Cicéron, Brutus. Si cette simplicité nous semble rudesse, si elle nous semble prématurée, ajournons-la, mais ajournons aussi la république."
2. *Archives Parlementaires*, LIII (Oct. 27, 1792), 18–19; LIII (Oct. 29, 1792), 36, 59; Desmoulins on the same decree argues for imitation of Cato and Collatinus, LIII (Oct. 29, 1792), 61.
3. *Annales patriotiques et littéraires*, No. 277 (Oct. 3, 1792), p. 1236.
4. *Archives Parlementaires*, LIII (Oct. 30, 1792), 77–8.
5. *Idem*, LIII (Nov. 13, 1792), 390; LV (Dec. 16, 1792), 79, 82.
6. *Idem*, LV (Dec. 16, 1792), 80. This speech is also noted by Eugène Maron, *Histoire littéraire de la convention nationale* (Paris, 1860), pp. 17–18.
7. *Archives Parlementaires*, LV (Dec. 16, 1792), 80–1.
8. *Prelude*, x, 96–120.
9. For classical allusions in Louvet's speech of accusation, see *Archives Parlementaires*, LIII (Oct. 29, 1792), 53, 56, 57, 58.

ing of Louvet in 1796 was under the direction of her more experienced brother.[1]

Incidentally, it should be noted that when Wordsworth returned to England he did not thereby escape revolutionary interpretations of ancient history. Mme. Roland's *Mémoires* also formed a part of the reading done at Racedown.[2] Like Louvet she was notably a child of the ancients. In her *Mémoires* she dates her republican sentiments from her earliest reading of Plutarch,[3] and she frequently imagines the life she might have led during the glorious days of ancient Greece.[4] But finally in the bitterness of her imprisonment she develops a passion for Tacitus[5] and comes to understand the terrible years of Tiberius which form the work of the Latin historian.[6]

In England, too, Wordsworth found British patriots adopting Roman ways. Coleridge's addresses of 1795, "On the Girondists" and "On the Present War," are titled *Conciones ad Populum,* and they are not without their classical allusions.[7] John Thelwall, who was on intimate terms with Coleridge from 1796 onward and who visited Wordsworth and Coleridge in July, 1797,[8] offers the most striking example of an Englishman using ancient history after the French manner. In 1796 when the Convention Bill prevented his direct attacks upon the British Government, he immediately resorted to lectures on Roman history. In these lectures, which were delivered in the country as well as in London, he continued to expound republican principles, merely shifting the point of application from modern England to ancient Rome.[9] Like the French and, ultimately, like Wordsworth, Thelwall found an intimate connection between virtue and republican institutions.[10]

The use of Roman history which was made by French and English republicans has here been briefly sketched. It is in itself a phenomenon of modern history. Because it formed the experience of countless men, it cannot be fully understood when it is considered from the point of view of a single individual—even if that individual be Wordsworth. Actually, my study of the phenomenon has been severely limited; I have hoped merely to indicate the ferment of ideas in which Wordsworth took some part. For this reason I have referred to the historical studies of only two *philosophes*—Montesquieu and Rousseau; I have arbitrarily selected Brissot and Louvet from among the many Girondists whose works Wordsworth would have known;

---

1. *EL*, p. 152.   2. *Ibid.*
3. *Mémoires de Madame Roland,* C. A. Dauban, éd. (Paris, 1864), pp. 16, 133.
4. *Idem,* pp. 76, 92.   5. *Idem,* p. 181.   6. *Idem,* p. 386.
7. Samuel Taylor Coleridge, *Conciones ad Populum* (1795), pp. 41, 52.
8. Charles Cestre, *John Thelwall: A Pioneer of Democracy and Social Reform* (London, 1906), pp. 140–4.
9. *Idem,* pp. 126–9.   10. *Idem,* pp. 57–8, 60.

and, finally, I have examined in a cursory way the contemporary records of only three months during Wordsworth's year in France. Obviously, the evidence of Roman thought which appears in these sources must be regarded as merely representative of a much larger body of material which Wordsworth undoubtedly knew.

The effect of the revolutionary use of Roman history which concerns us here is the effect that it had on Wordsworth's reading. This effect can be briefly stated—and largely in Wordsworth's own words. When he went to France he was "almost indifferent" to political thought,

> ... even the historian's tale
> Prizing but little otherwise than I prized
> Tales of the poets, as it made the heart
> Beat high, and filled the fancy with fair forms,
> Old heroes and their sufferings and their deeds.[2]

But, after his schooling with Beaupuy, he

> ... bore a sounder judgment
> Than later days allowed; carried about me,
> With less alloy to its integrity,
> The experience of past ages, as, through help
> Of books and common life, it makes sure way
> To youthful minds, by objects over near
> Not pressed upon, nor dazzled or misled
> By struggling with the crowd for present ends.[3]

In France he learned that history, and particularly the ancient history of Rome, could be made to serve "present ends." History had come to life as it never could have done had there been no further introduction than the examinations of St. John's. When he settled down to serious, independent study and began to devote twelve hours of thought to society to every one to poetry,[4] he naturally followed the examples of the political leaders whom he knew. He went to the Romans to learn polity or to find support for the principles he already held.

Independence characterizes Wordsworth's mature study of Roman historical and political writers, for although he entered Rome with a goodly company he chose to remain and explore alone. What he made of the experience will be shown in the following chapter. The present business is to observe his respect for learning and to discover what authors he knew and how well he knew them.

Many years ago Professor Lane Cooper manfully defended Words-

---

2. *Prelude*, IX, 204–08.   3. *Idem*, IX, 332–9.
4. See W. H. White, *An Examination of the Charge of Apostasy against Wordsworth* (London and New York, 1898), p. 16.

worth from the ridiculous charges of being a poet untouched by books.[5] Since that time most modern scholars have come to share Professor Cooper's view that Wordsworth read widely and often with serious intent.[6] Certainly it is true that Wordsworth's poetry and letters testify to a sincere love of study:

> Dreams, books, are each a world; and books, we know,
> Are a substantial world, both pure and good:
> Round these, with tendrils strong as flesh and blood,
> Our pastime and our happiness will grow.[7]

In his letters references to reading are countless.[8] There we discover among other things that the reading at Racedown progressed with a "usual regularity,"[9] that proximity to a good library always determined his choice of residence,[1] that he often commissioned friends in London or abroad to search the book markets, and also that before he entered upon his most ambitious tasks he read for the "nourishment of his mind."[2] These are the habits of a man truly attached to book learning.

Wordsworth often acquired his books through the help of friends. Lamb and De Quincey first bought for him,[3] and later Crabb Robinson and Landor.[4] For example, in 1808 Dorothy Wordsworth sent his current requests to De Quincey: William wants particularly "Clarendon—Burnet—any of the elder Histories—translations from the Classics chiefly historical—Plutarch's Lives—Thucydides, Tacitus (I think he said), (by the bye, he *has* a translation of Herodotus), Lord Bacon's Works—Milton's Prose . . ."[10] The next year De Quincey himself moved to Grasmere and brought almost thirty chests of books with him—much to the delight of his neighbours.[11] But, re-

---

5. Lane Cooper, "A Glance at Wordsworth's Reading," *Modern Language Notes*, XXII (1907), 83–9, 110–17.
6. De Selincourt, *Prelude*, pp. xxviii–xxx; Arthur Beatty, ed., *Wordsworth: Representative Poems* (New York, 1937), p. xxvii; Douglas Bush, *Mythology and the Romantic Tradition in English Poetry* (Cambridge, 1937), pp. 56–7; Havens, *op. cit.*, pp. 351–2.
7. "Personal Talk," ll. 33–6. See also *Prelude*, I, 114–18; III, 367–8; IV-A, 281–2; V, 38 ff.; V-A, 630–3; VI, 95–114; IX, 28–33; XIV, 312–13. *Excursion*, I, 83; IV, 564–70.
8. For example, see *EL*, pp. 49, 51, 128, 253.
9. *Idem*, p. 151.
1. *Idem*, pp. 193, 228. See also a letter of Coleridge to Thomas Poole, May, 1799: Coleridge refused to leave Alfoxden—"W. was affected *to tears*, very much affected; but he deemed the vicinity of a library absolutely *necessary* to his health, nay to his existence" (*Letters of Samuel Taylor Coleridge*, Ernest Hartley Coleridge, ed. [London, 1895, 2 vols.], I, 297).
2. *EL*, p. 561.
3. See *The Works of Charles and Mary Lamb*, E. V. Lucas, ed. (London, 1903–05, 7 vols.), VI, 289, 294–5; VII, 912. See also *MY*, I, 233–4.
4. See *The Correspondence of Henry Crabb Robinson with the Wordsworth Circle*, Edith J. Morley, ed. (Oxford, 1927, 2 vols.), I, 298; John Forster, *Walter Savage Landor* (London, 1869, 2 vols.), II, 115–17; *LY*, I, 133–4.
10. *MY*, I, 233.   11. *Idem*, I, 346.

gardless of the advantages of borrowing, Wordsworth continued to spend all the money he could spare from his meager income on old books.[7] As he became more affluent, he enriched his library proportionately. Whereas Lamb had sent single volumes, Robinson and Landor sent packages and boxes. Many of the later additions were gifts—unto everyone that hath shall be given. Landor, of course, was an experienced buyer of classical books, and some of Wordsworth's rarest items bear Landor's inscription.[8] Although Landor speaks of sending Wordsworth "small" packages, it is difficult to grasp his notion of a "small" package. One shipment to Southey, admittedly a larger shipment than any to Wordsworth, contained 22 folios, 13 quartos, and 41 smaller books.[9]

One of the most difficult documents I have had to deal with in my search for information about Wordsworth's reading is *The Rydal Mount Library Catalogue*. The difficulties are manifold: for instance, books are listed in lots with single volumes often going under such provocative titles as *Et cetera, Et cetera;* also there is no way of telling when most of the books were acquired; finally, the catalogue is a catalogue not of the library, but only of the sale of 1859 from which the family withheld many books.[1] Family records and later sale catalogues provide answers to some questions,[2] but even so the conclusions to be drawn about Wordsworth's library are necessarily limited.

One conclusion which is certainly safe to make is that over a period of years Wordsworth acquired a substantial collection of Roman historical and political writers. Of these writers Cicero is the one most conspicuously represented in number alone. In *The Rydal Mount Library Catalogue* seven items are specifically named,[3] while an eighth goes under the elusive title of "Cicero (Latin)";[4] several of these items are various editions of the same work. In a catalogue made by Dora in 1829, the titles of four separate works are mentioned, and the list is completed with two references to *Ciceronis Opera*, one reference bearing the description—" 10 vol: qto."[5]

7. *Idem*, II, 487.
8. *Rydal Mount*, Lots 14, 288, 591.
9. John Forster, *op. cit.*, II, 118–9.
1. See preface to *Transactions of the Wordsworth Society* (Edinburgh), No. 6, p. iv.
2. See, for example, "Books from Wordsworth's Library," *The Athenaeum*, No. 3579 (May 30, 1896), p. 714; W. Roberts, "Wordsworth as a Book Collector," *Literature*, VI (May 19, 1900), 383–4; *Times Literary Supplement* (Notes on Sales), May 27, 1920; *The Official Catalogue of the Contents of Dove Cottage* (Ambleside, 1922), pp. 39–40; *The Correspondence of Henry Crabb Robinson*, II, 867–74; L. N. Broughton, *The Wordsworth Collection* (Cornell University Library, 1931), and *The Wordsworth Collection: A Supplement to the Catalogue* (Ithaca, 1942); C. H. Patton, *The Amherst Wordsworth Collection* (1936); two Harvard University MSS. ("Catalogue of Wordsworth's Library in the Hand of His Daughter" in the Houghton Library, and "Account of Books Lent from the Library at Rydal Mount" in the Harry Elkins Widener Collection).
3. Lots 346, 347, 348, 350, 383, 564, 579.
4. Lot 348.
5. Harvard University MS., pp. 1–2, 92.

To go from Cicero to Caesar is to go from one extreme to another Records of Wordsworth's library mention only one edition of Caesar, and that only the *Gallic Wars*. Bibliographically it is perhaps more remarkable than any of the editions of Cicero, and it well becomes the presentation autograph of Walter Savage Landor.[6] The autograph, of course, indicates that it was a late acquisition.

Tacitus is well represented—both numerically and bibliographically. The complete works appear once in the Elzevir edition of 1649,[7] once in an Ernesti edition (1752, 1772?),[8] once in a French translation,[9] and once in the famous Tudor translation of Sir Henry Savile.[1] There is also an Italian edition of Tacitus entitled *Reflessioni Morali*.[2]

Compared with Tacitus, Livy makes a poor showing. He is mentioned only once and the edition is not described.[3] It is quite possible that some of Wordsworth's knowledge of Livy's first decade came through Machiavelli. Wordsworth several times speaks of Machiavelli as a profound and noble statesman;[4] in Wordsworth's estimation *The Discourse upon Livius*, of which he owned an English translation,[5] might well have taken precedence over *The Prince*.

Plutarch also appears only once. Like so many English poets Wordsworth apparently read Plutarch in North's translation. His copy is a folio edition of 1676. In *The Rydal Mount Library Catalogue* the volume is inaccurately cited,[10] and the error has led De Selincourt to imagine that Wordsworth read Plutarch in "the French translation of Thevet."[11] Besides North's translations of the *Lives*, the volume includes "The lives of twenty selected eminent persons . . . translated out of the work of that famous historiographer to the King of France and Poland; Andrew Thevet." Thevet was apparently a man with many interests; his eminent persons range from Aristotle to Sappho to Edward Prince of Wales to Tamerlane to Gutenberg.

Like Plutarch, another Greek writer important in Wordsworth's study of Roman history is represented only in translation. Polybius appears in a translation done by Edward Grimeston, Sergeant at Armes (1634).[12] According to the title page the translation was made from the Greek original, and it has been accepted as such by bibliog-

---

6. *Rydal Mount*, Lot 14.   7. *Idem*, Lot 410.
8. Harvard University MS. ("Catalogue of Wordsworth's Library in the Hand of His Daughter"), p. 6.
9. *Rydal Mount*, Lot 75.
1. *The Athenaeum*, No. 3579 (May 30, 1896), p. 714.
2. *Rydal Mount*, Lot 441.
3. *Idem*, Lot 348. The catalogue in the hand of Dora offers little help; her entry is simply "Livii Histor: 2nd Vol., Livius ———. 1st Vol." (Harvard University MS., p. 4).
4. *EL*, p. 122; *MY*, II, 748; *LY*, III, 1335.
5. *Rydal Mount*, Lot 44.
10. Lot 77.   11. *Prelude*, p. 504.   12. *Rydal Mount*, Lot 60.

raphers.[9] But actually all that Grimeston did was to make a *word for word* translation from the French Polybius of Louis Maigret.[1] If Grimeston had hoped to make a translation out of Maigret comparable to North's translation of Amyot, he was overly sanguine. The prose is as bad as could be expected.

Other editions and translations owned by Wordsworth indicate his remarkably wide interest in Roman history. In *The Rydal Mount Library Catalogue* are single copies of Cassius Dio (in a French translation), of Florus, and of Herodian (printed with a Latin translation facing the original Greek), and two copies of Valerius Maximus.[2] Notable figures in the catalogue made by Dora Wordsworth are Suetonius, Sallust, Cornelius Nepos, and Velleius Paterculus.[3] Worth noticing are other classical works indirectly related to Roman history: for example, Quintus Rufus' history of Alexander the Great; Pomponius Mela's *De Situ Orbis,* which bears the autographs of both Coleridge and Wordsworth; Strabo's *Geographica* in the recension of Isaac Casaubon.[4] There are also classic anthologies and selections, school texts on Roman antiquities, and finally the English Gibbon.[5]

This brief description of the Rydal Mount library raises an important question about Wordsworth's reading in classical literature. Did he read the classics in the original or in translation? Judging from the books which he owned and from the quotations he made, I believe that it was for Wordsworth a matter of indifference whether he read *Latin prose* in the original or in translation. His knowledge of Latin can be briefly summed up. When he left Cambridge he declared in a mood of self-reproach that he knew "little of Latin and scarce anything of Greek."[6] If such a statement were true (his self-conscious manner suggests a certain amount of exaggeration), the deficiency was soon remedied. His translations of Latin poetry[7] and his frequent

9. Henrietta R. Palmer, *List of English Editions and Translations of Greek and Latin Classics before 1641* (London, 1911), p. 91; W. T. Lowndes, *The Bibliographer's Manual of English Literature* (Revised and enlarged edition by Henry G. Bohn, London, 1890), IV, 1909; Basil Anderton and T. E. Turnbull, *Catalogue of Books Concerning the Greek and Latin Classics* (Newcastle-upon-Tyne, 1912), p. 201.

1. Grimeston used the second edition of Maigret (*Les Cinq Premiers livres des histoires de Polybe* . . . Autrefois traduits & mis en lumiere par Louis Maigret . . . Ausquelz de nouveau sont ajoutees les subsequentes Parcelles des livres IX . . . XVII, toutes traduites par lui sur l'exemplaire Grec. A Lion. 1558). In translating everything (marginalia, annotated maps, etc.) Grimeston also translated the epistle of Maigret to the French nobility, and perhaps he intended thereby to indicate his obligation to the French.

2. Lots 533, 445, 40, 410.   3. Harvard University MS., pp. 2–6.
4. *Rydal Mount,* Lots 410, 141, 160.
5. *Idem,* Lots 40, 365, 67, 237, 29. (Gibbon's *Decline and Fall* was apparently not acquired until 1836; see *The Correspondence of Henry Crabb Robinson,* I, 298.)
6. *EL,* p. 61.
7. See above, p. 3; "Translation of part of the First Book of the Æneid," "Imitation

testimony to an "intimate" knowledge of the Latin poets[8] show a reformed spirit. De Quincey's judgment is probably the right one. He said that Wordsworth "by reading the lyric poetry of Horace, simply for his own delight as a student of composition, made himself a master of Latinity in its most difficult form."[9]

But, if we accept De Quincey's verdict on Wordsworth's knowledge of Latin, ought we not also to accept his less favorable verdict on Wordsworth's knowledge of Greek? "As to Greek, that is a language which Wordsworth never had energy enough to cultivate with effect."[1] Certainly Wordsworth had some knowledge of Greek,[2] but it was not an "intimate" knowledge such as he had of Latin and it was not exercised in the reading of Greek prose. A significant indication of Wordsworth's reading in Greek is the fact that practically all the Greek prose writers whose works he possessed were represented only in translation.[3]

In a study of Wordsworth's reading, the ideal would be to use the texts which he used. But from the description of the Latin authors in his library it is obvious that such an ideal is impossible to achieve. For example, Tacitus presents a choice of two Latin editions, a French translation, an English translation; Livy offers no choice. In view of these difficulties it has seemed best to me to select standard Latin texts of today. Since my study does not depend upon textual criticism of either Wordsworth or the Latins, there is no reason not to use modern editions. To make selections for the Greek authors has been comparatively easy. Wordsworth owned single copies of Plutarch and Polybius, and apparently read Greek prose only in translation. It is logical, therefore, to study at least these writers in the translations used by Wordsworth.

From a knowledge of Wordsworth's library, other conclusions about his reading may be drawn. First, he owned a collection of Roman historical and political writers which enabled him, if he wished, to acquire a remarkably wide knowledge of Roman antiquity. Secondly, his collection indicates a real interest in Roman history; either Wordsworth himself bought the works of Roman writers or his friends recognized his interest and gave thoughtfully. It is true, of course, that the best-laid schemes gang aft agley, and perhaps none more than schemes for a self-imposed discipline.

---

of Juvenal—Satire VIII" in *The Poetical Works of William Wordsworth* (Oxford, 1940), pp. 302–06.
8. *LY*, I, 70; *Prose Works*, III, 458–9.
9. *The Collected Writings of Thomas De Quincey*, v, 204.
1. *Idem*, II, 265.
2. See *MY*, II, 487; *LY*, I, 194; "Wordsworth and Greek," *Notes and Queries*, CLXXVII (Nov. 18, 1939), 366–7.
3. For example, see *Rydal Mount*, Lots 41, 107, 408, 409.

For further evidence of Wordsworth's reading it is necessary, therefore, to turn to more authoritative sources. Such sources are his own direct references to the classic writers. These references are few, but it should be remembered that Wordsworth was not given to long intimate correspondence and that his poetry did not lend itself to essays on criticism. In his letters are scattered references to Polybius,[4] Cicero,[5] Livy,[6] Nepos,[7] and Tacitus,[8] and one quotation from Florus.[9] I have already quoted in part a letter of Dorothy Wordsworth's conveying a request of her brother's for translations of Tacitus and Plutarch, but in his own letters Wordsworth makes no reference to Plutarch.

It is in his poetry that he testifies more fully to a reading of Roman prose—and of Plutarch in particular. Plutarch's life of Dion is the source for Wordsworth's narrative poem on the same hero; Plutarch's life of Flamininus, together perhaps with portions of Livy's later history, is the source for two of Wordsworth's political sonnets; again, it was probably Plutarch's life of Sertorius that inspired Wordsworth with the desire to write a long narrative poem:

>   . . . how the friends
> And followers of Sertorius, out of Spain
> Flying, found shelter in the Fortunate Isles,
> And left their usages, their arts and laws,
> To disappear by a slow gradual death,
> To dwindle and to perish one by one,
> Starved in those narrow bounds: but not the soul
> Of Liberty . . .[1]

Wordsworth's poetic allusions to Arminius, Viriathus, Numa, Lucius and Marcus Brutus, Timoleon, Caligula[2] show a knowledge of Roman history which is based on more than the traditional accounts to be found in English literature. The same knowledge leads him to set up Phocion, Epaminondas, and Philopoemen as models for the military generals of his own day[3] and to find in the Senate's reception of Terentius Varro "the sublimest event in human history."[10] In contemplating scenes of particular historic interest Wordsworth occasionally conveys something of his unique feeling for Roman history.

4. *MY*, I, 443.
5. *LY*, II, 876. See also *Memorials of a Tour in Italy, 1837*, I, 254.
6. *LY*, II, 860.   7. *MY*, II, 487.   8. *LY*, I, 276.   9. *MY*, I, 439.
1. *Prelude*, I, 190–7.
2. See *A Concordance to the Poems of William Wordsworth*, Lane Cooper, ed. (London, 1911).
3. *Prose Works*, I, 75 ("The Convention of Cintra").
10. *MY*, I, 439.

> Imagination feels what Reason fears not
> To recognize, the lasting virtue lodged
> In those bold fictions that, by deeds assigned
> To the Valerian, Fabian, Curian Race,
> And others like in fame, created Powers
> With attributes from History derived,
> By Poesy irradiate, and yet graced,
> Through marvellous felicity of skill,
> With something more propitious to high aims
> Than either, pent within her separate sphere,
> Can oft with justice claim.[5]

Lines such as these indicate a genuine love of Roman history; their full significance should become more apparent after a study of the Roman influences upon Wordsworth's thought and work.

---

5. *Memorials of a Tour in Italy, 1837*, I, 278–88; see also XII, XIII ("Near the Lake of Thrasymene"), and *Prelude*, XI, 376–83.

II

Roman Influence on Wordsworth's Political Thought

"Moribus antiquis res stat Romana virisque."

ENNIUS.

IN his political thought Wordsworth put general principles before party affiliation, before political expediency, before the interests of economics and sociology. Early and late he claimed to have "stuck to *Principles*."[1] In 1794 when he joined his college friend William Mathews in laying plans for a periodical publication, he urged that they "let slip no opportunity of explaining and enforcing those general principles of the social order, which are applicable to all times and to all places."[2] In 1809 after completing his political tract on the Convention of Cintra, he confessed that the convention was after all "an action dwelt upon only for the sake of illustrating principles, with a view to promote liberty and good policy."[3] In 1816 he spoke of a representative political sonnet as a poem embodying "certain principles of action which human nature has thousands of times proved herself capable of being governed by."[4] Fifteen years later he echoed the early Wordsworth in insisting that "Sound minds find their expediency in principles."[5] In 1834 principles are still "the only things worth contending about."[6]

It is the first aim of this chapter to prove that many of these general principles, which constitute the essence of Wordsworth's political thought, either take their source or find illustration and support in the historical and political writing of ancient Rome. In other words, I believe that Roman history contributed to Wordsworth's political thought either by suggesting new principles or by providing evidence to justify principles which had been acquired by other means.

It is important in any study of Wordsworth's political philosophy to recognize the distinction between principles and the application of principles. W. H. White and A. V. Dicey have both argued well for the essential consistency in Wordsworth's political thought; in so far as they have succeeded, they have done so by concentrating on his principles alone.[7] To carry further the argument for political con-

---

1. *LY*, I, 56.   2. *EL*, p. 120.   3. *MY*, I, 264.   4. *Idem*, II, 711.
5. *LY*, II, 591.   6. *Idem*, II, 704.
7. White, *An Examination of the Charge of Apostasy against Wordsworth*; A. V. Dicey, *The Statesmanship of Wordsworth* (Oxford, 1917).

sistency seems to me impossible. In *The Later Wordsworth* Miss Batho made a valiant attempt; but, to resolve the differences between Wordsworth the Revolutionary and Wordsworth the Tory, she had to resort to a labored argument.[8] As I see it, Wordsworth's political *theory* remained consistent because he did, in fact, "stick to *Principles.*" But his opinions on contemporary problems changed radically over a period of years, and as a result his political allegiances changed quite as radically.

The dichotomy of his politics requires that principles and practices be considered separately. In this study, therefore, I shall consider the influence of Roman history, first, upon the political principles of Wordsworth and, secondly, upon his application of those principles. For it is the second aim of this chapter to show that Roman history exercised some influence—for better or for worse—upon Wordsworth's practical politics.

Wordsworth's insistence upon morality in art, government, and human relationships does much to explain his love for the classic historians. It was as if Roman history had been written to order for the political poet who insisted upon moral purposes.[9] Without a single exception the Romans whom Wordsworth knew best all confessed in their major works a didactic purpose.

Polybius over and over again argues that "there is no way more easie to reforme and better Men, then the Knowledge of things past."[1] He believes that the experience of the past offers the soundest and most sensible discipline for the present,[2] and he, therefore, writes his history with the idea of presenting to posterity wisdom acquired through a study of centuries of political experience.

Livy and Plutarch phrase the same sentiment. In the preface to his great history of Rome, Livy proclaims that the chief value of history lies in the wealth of examples it offers for moral and political behavior.[3] Throughout the whole of his history he consciously offers for emulation the noble actions of his best Romans. In Plutarch we find perhaps the most pleasing statements of moral purpose. Plutarch explains that he chooses not to write formal history because in the great sweep of military and political affairs the virtues and vices of individual men are often lost sight of.[4] He writes instead single biographies, emphasizing the virtues for the sake of imitation: "For such effects doth vertue bring: that either to hear or read them, they do print in our hearts an earnest love and desire to follow them."[5] In

---

8. Edith C. Batho, *The Later Wordsworth* (Cambridge, 1933), pp. 119–233.
9. For Wordsworth's insistence upon moral purposes, see *EL*, pp. 295–8; *MY*, I, 128.
1. Polybius, p. 1. 2. *Idem*, p. 25. 3. Livy, I, Praef. 10.
4. Plutarch, p. 559 (Alexander the Great).
5. *Idem*, p. 132 (Pericles).

the introduction to his life of Aemilius Paullus he charmingly confesses that he himself has felt the better for his association with the great men of history.[6]

Tacitus, no less than the others, adopts a moral purpose in his histories. In a way he even enlarges the didactic power of history into a positive force for good in present as well as future society. Recognizing fame as the last infirmity of noble mind, Tacitus attempts to turn the weakness to a good account. History, which by its very nature commemorates the most striking examples of noble behavior, urges men to virtue; and at the same time it threatens the evildoer with the disapproval of future generations.[7]

The emphasis put upon moral virtue by classic historians marks them as philosophers teaching by example. The work of the classic historian may be praised with that of the poet. "Quam multas nobis imagines non solum ad intuendum, verum etiam ad imitandum fortissimorum virorum expressas scriptores et Graeci et Latini reliquerunt."[8]

The concrete examples of history would inevitably have attracted Wordsworth to history in general. As Dicey has pointed out, Wordsworth in his political thought was "always coming back to realities,"[9] and next to experience itself history offered the political poet the largest field of reality. But it was the moral purposes apparent in Roman history that made Wordsworth put classic history first. In Livy or Plutarch he could find that quality of mind which he prized so highly:

> The glorious habit by which sense is made
> Subservient still to moral purposes,
> Auxiliar to divine.[1]

The modern historians who write of "power and energy detached From moral purpose"[2] are, he tells us, comparatively worthless; indeed, the more scientific and incredulous they become, the more deplorable is their work.[3]

Since a moral purpose directed in large part the work of the classic historian, it followed as a natural consequence that his political principles were essentially *moral* principles. One of the most common of these principles was that a good government depends mainly upon the virtue of the people. So long as the people remain virtuous—observing the classic rules of justice, temperance, courage, and prudence—so long will their government remain secure and good. But, when

---

6. *Idem*, p. 205.
7. Tacitus, *Ann*., III, 65. See also Tacitus, *Hist*., III, 51; Tacitus, *Agr*., I, 1–3.
8. Cicero, *Pro Archia Poeta*, VI, 14, in *The Speeches*, N. H. Watts, ed. and tr. (Loeb Classical Library, 1935).
9. Dicey, *op. cit.*, p. 15.　　1. *Excursion*, IV, 1247–9.　　2. *Prelude*, XIII, 43–4.
3. See *Memorials of a Tour in Italy, 1837*, IV–VI.

moral discipline is relaxed, correspondent changes occur in the government, and despotisms of one kind or another begin to take root. (It is no wonder that the office of censor was in Rome an office of peculiar dignity and power.)[4]

This principle of political theory is so unanimously supported by the Romans that their histories fairly swarm with examples. To begin with one of the earliest writers: in his famous book on the Constitution of Rome, Polybius defines the six classic forms of government. He analyzes the three forms of government which can for a period of time exercise a just rule: kingship, aristocracy, and democracy. But these three forms, existing separately, are regularly perverted into tyranny, oligarchy, or mob rule. In every case Polybius finds that the cause which works a change from good to bad government is a moral cause. The rulers become drunk with power, insolent, and despotic; the ruled become envious, inordinate, and avaricious, until finally a change for the worse becomes unavoidable.[5]

When the Roman historians write of legendary Rome and of the early Republic, they all credit its good fortune to the virtues of its citizens. Livy and Plutarch both examine the legislation of early Rome for its moral effects, believing that sound morality was the sole aim of ancient lawgivers.[6] Sallust,[7] Livy,[8] Plutarch,[9] Florus,[1] all insist that the high moral character of early Rome accounts for all its greatness, and at the same time the Latin writers look upon the wickedness of their own day as the chief cause of all civic misfortune.

Tacitus accepts the poetic tradition of a Golden Age; he holds that at first men were all naturally good and, therefore, blessed with good government: "At postquam exui aequalitas et pro modestia ac pudore ambitio et vis incedebat, provenere dominationes multosque apud populos aeternum mansere."[2] Although Tacitus describes minutely the wickedness of various emperors, he does not allow the entire blame for evil days to be shifted upon them. He shows that the Senate so invited shame and degradation that even Tiberius himself was disgusted.[3] Later in his narrative of Piso's conspiracy, he emphasizes the degeneracy which, like a disease, has spread through Roman nobility.[10] Indeed, the closing years of Augustus' reign and the general

---

4. On the office of censor, see Cicero, *De Legibus*, III, iii, 7; Livy, IV, viii, 2–7; Plutarch, pp. 295–6 (Marcus Cato).
5. Polybius, pp. 283–7. Cf. J. B. Bury, *The Ancient Greek Historians* (New York, 1909), p. 219.
6. Livy, I, XIX; Plutarch, pp. 54, 58–9 (Numa).   7. Sallust, *Bell Cat*, IX and X.
8. Livy, I, Praef. 9; IV, vi, 11–12; VII, xl, 2; X, ix, 5–6.
9. Plutarch, pp. 50–62 (Numa, *passim*).
1. Florus, I, xvii.   2. Tacitus, *Ann*, III, 26.   3. *Ann*, III, 65.
10. See *Ann*, XV, 48, 57. Gaston Boissier, *Tacitus and Other Roman Studies*, W. G. Hutchison, tr. (New York, 1906), p. 142, thinks that Tacitus consciously contrasts the weaknesses of the nobility with the strength of Epicharis the freedwoman.

acceptance of empire as a *fait accompli* marked for Tacitus not so much the beginning of a new political era as the end of all sound morality.[5]

The moral Plutarch praises the work of legislators who recognize the close connection between private morality and public safety. Lycurgus is probably his most striking example. According to Plutarch the reforms of Lycurgus were directed by moral, rather than economic or political, principles:

> . . . he thought the felicity of a City, as of a private man, consisted chiefly in the exercise of vertue, and in the unity of the Inhabitants thereof. He framed his Common-wealth to this end, that his Citizens should be nobly minded, content with their own, and temperate in their doings, that thereby they might maintain and keep themselves long in safety.[6]

Moral discipline thus accounts for the flourishing good fortune of the Spartan state, and, conversely, a relaxation of that discipline explains its later misfortunes. Lysander allowed gold and silver to be introduced into the public transactions of the Spartan state; but at the same time he continued to enforce the law of Lycurgus which required the people to conduct their private business with *iron* currency. Plutarch reproaches Lysander and his party for adding a kind of official dignity to the very object they wanted despised by the people. He then goes on to add an interesting comment on the connection between public and private virtues:

> . . . we are rather to think, that private mens manners are confirmed according to the common uses and customs of Cities, then that the faults and vices of private men do fill Cities and Commonweales with ill qualities. And it is more likely, that the parts are marred and corrupted with an infection of the whole, when it falleth out ill: then that the parts corrupted should draw the whole to corruption.[7]

When we turn to the political theories of Cicero we find the same emphasis on virtue as the chief source of good government. In *De Legibus* Cicero maintains that the establishment of a sound political state is the whole aim of his discourse.[8] He then pursues this aim by attacking problems of ethics.[9] Although the second book of *The Laws* deals with religious laws, the problems remain essentially ethical. The state is apparently concerned in religious laws not so much out of fear of the gods as out of fear of its own people; so long as the people are virtuous, the state is healthy, but, once they become de-

---

5. Tacitus, *Ann*, I, 4: "verso civitatis statu nihil usquam prisci et integri moris."
6. Plutarch, p. 49.   7. *Idem*, pp. 378–9 (Lysander).
8. Cicero, *De Legibus*, I, xiii, 37.
9. See, for example, his comment on the law that the senate should set an example for the rest of the state (*idem*, III, xiii, 30 to xiv, 32).

generate, the constitution of the ideal republic is as nothing. It is for this reason that Cicero attends to whatever may contribute to improving the morals of the citizens. For example, he observes that the religious music of his own time has become immoderate and acts as a debilitating influence. He recalls the wisdom of the Greeks in forbidding such inordinate performances; though he doubts the efficacy of such a law for his own time, he commends them for recognizing that corruption in the hearts of citizens will eventually overturn the whole state.[1]

Since the Romans all agreed that virtue alone assures good government, it is not surprising to find that they also agreed in believing that only the virtuous could enjoy civil liberty. Liberty was after all a consequence of good government and likewise depended upon the virtue of the people. A good government would have good laws; that is, laws to lead men to a more virtuous life. In obeying such laws, the Romans found their liberty. "Legum denique idcirco omnes servi sumus, ut liberi esse possimus."[2]

Because the Romans looked back upon the early days of the Republic as the happiest time of Rome's history, it was natural that they should discover in the Republic the greatest amount of liberty.[3] And they recognized that that liberty existed only because the people were fit for it. Livy made much of this point.[4] He showed how the early reigns had contributed to the moral preparation for liberty, and he believed that Brutus could not successfully have acted any sooner than he did. When the Tarquins were expelled, the Roman people had been brought to just the right pitch for liberty.[5] In the same way Livy recognized that liberty among the corrupt was simply a form of license and an indication of an insecure government.[6] Tacitus' acceptance of the empire was probably due in large part to his belief that the Romans were no longer morally capable of enjoying liberty.[7]

The principle that virtue alone makes for a happy state and its concomitant that only the virtuous may enjoy civil liberty are fundamental to Wordsworth's political thought. The tract on the Convention of Cintra provides the most succinct expression of the main principle: "In the moral virtues and qualities of passion which belong to a people, must the ultimate salvation of a people be sought for."[8]

1. *Idem,* II, xv, 38–9.
2. Cicero, *Pro Cluentio,* LIII, 146, in *The Speeches,* H. G. Hodge, ed. and tr. (Loeb Classical Library, 1927).
3. See Tacitus, *Ann,* I, i; III, 27; Cicero, *De Legibus,* II, x, 23.
4. Livy, II, i, 3–7. See also Livy's comments on the loss of liberty under the Decemvirs: III, xxxvii, 1–3.
5. *Idem,* II, i, 6.   6. *Idem,* XXIII, ii, 1 to iv, 8.
7. See Galba's address to Piso, *Hist.,* I, 16: "'imperaturus es hominibus qui nec totam servitutem pati possunt nec totam libertatem.'"
8. *Prose Works,* I, 49; see also I, 40.

Throughout the whole tract Wordsworth insists over and over again that the Spanish must place all their hopes in the exercise of virtue.[9] Even the practical help which they may hope to enlist from the British depends in its turn upon the moral character of their ally. To accomplish real assistance the English had first to feel in their actions "an origination and direction unquestionably moral."[1]

Wordsworth's letters offer other examples of his faith in the virtue of a people as the chief power of a state.[2] Of these the most important for its direct use of Roman history is a letter to Captain Pasley, March 28, 1811. Wordsworth again puts all his hope for Europe "upon moral influence, and the wishes and opinions of the people of the respective nations."[3] The example of the Romans emboldens him in this hope. In Rome's defeat of the Carthaginians Wordsworth believes the most active force for victory to have been not military power but rather "civic fortitude."[4] And, conversely, he reminds his correspondent that, when Rome was disgraced by the rebellion of Spartacus, the total resources of a vast empire were hardly sufficient to win the day.[5] Wordsworth is here strictly in Roman fashion: he finds the virtue of the early Republic the source of its strength, while on the other hand he finds the material strength of the Empire insufficient to sustain the corruption at home.

But, of course, the most interesting expressions of this principle occur in his poetry. His comments on the French Revolution, both in *The Prelude* and in *The Excursion,* present frequent illustration. In *The Prelude* Wordsworth describes the faith he had once held for the success of the French Revolution—a faith founded upon signs of a coming moral regeneration.[6] The monarchy of France, which had built up "a terrific reservoir of guilt And ignorance," was naturally perishable;[7] the true "Wealth of Nations," permanent and dependable, is lodged only in its virtuous men.[8] Wordsworth's later comments on the failure of the French Revolution are based on the same principle which had once given him cause for hope. In *The Excursion*

9. See also two sonnets of 1815, "Avaunt all specious pliancy of mind" and "O'erweening Statesmen have full long relied."
1. *Prose Works,* I, 41.
2. *MY,* I, 227 (Moral virtues are a better source of revenue than lotteries and distilleries!); II, 783–4.
3. *Idem,* I, 436.
4. *Idem,* I, 439. See also Wordsworth's letter (March, 1811), *idem,* I, 441–3, wherein he refers to Polybius' account of Hannibal's entry into Italy to illustrate the same point.
5. *Idem,* I, 439. Notice Wordsworth's quotation from Florus, II, viii, 12. Grosart's reference to Florus is erroneous (*Prose Works,* I, 359).
6. *Prelude,* IX, 385–9; XI, 11–12.
7. *Idem,* X, 477–8. Cf. *Prose Works,* I, 163: "every thing which is desperately immoral, being in its constitution monstrous, is of itself perishable" ("The Convention of Cintra").
8. *Prelude,* XIII, 76–100.

he still holds that the success of a social and political revolution depends upon its moral bias. He had been mistaken in supposing that the men of France would be zealous and consistent in the pursuit of virtue. But he still believes that, if they had been, the Revolution would then have succeeded, and, therefore, the principle for him remains the same.

> . . . the bad
> Have fairly earned a victory o'er the weak,
> The vacillating, inconsistent good.
> Therefore, not unconsoled, I wait—in hope
> To see the moment, when the righteous cause
> Shall gain defenders zealous and devout
> As they who have opposed her; in which Virtue
> Will, to her efforts, tolerate no bounds
> That are not lofty as her rights; aspiring
> By impulse of her own ethereal zeal.
> That spirit only can redeem mankind;
> And when that sacred spirit shall appear,
> Then shall *our* triumph be complete as theirs.[9]

That these lines were no mere poetic effusion, but rather the expression of an earnest, practical belief, is further argued by Wordsworth's use of identical language to present the same idea in his prose essay on the Cintra Convention. "When wickedness acknowledges no limit but the extent of her power . . . the only worthy or adequate opposition is—that of virtue submitting to no circumscription of her endeavours save that of her rights, and aspiring from the impulse of her own ethereal zeal."[1]

Not only does Wordsworth expect virtue to save the political man but also he looks to virtue to save the new scientific man. In this, of course, he would seem to go far beyond the Romans. But, actually, in one of his most striking passages on science and its relation to society, he chooses to hang the moral upon Archimedes, and in so doing he turns directly back to Cicero and Plutarch. The whole passage testifies to Wordsworth's faith in virtue and the moral law as the only hope for society, and for that reason alone the passage would be worth quoting. The Wanderer of *The Excursion* has commented upon the effects of the industrial revolution, deploring the unnatural existence it has forced upon workers, admiring the scientific achievements:

> ". . . all true glory rests,
> All praise, all safety, and all happiness,
> Upon the moral law. Egyptian Thebes,
> Tyre, by the margin of the sounding waves,

9. *Excursion*, IV, 307–19.   1. *Prose Works*, I, 170.

Palmyra, central in the desert, fell;
And the Arts died by which they had been raised.
—Call Archimedes from his buried tomb
Upon the grave of vanished Syracuse,
And feelingly the Sage shall make report
How insecure, how baseless in itself,
Is the Philosophy whose sway depends
On mere material instruments;—how weak
Those arts, and high inventions, if unpropped
By virtue.—He, sighing with pensive grief,
Amid his calm abstractions, would admit
That not the slender privilege is theirs
To save themselves from blank forgetfulness!"[2]

Besides the considered judgments on political affairs which occur in *The Prelude* and *The Excursion,* there are the impassioned addresses of Wordsworth's political sonnets. With the exception of two sonnets on Flamininus in Greece, none of these poems has a specific source in Roman prose. But almost every one expresses—often implicitly—that chief principle of Roman political thought which here concerns us. When Wordsworth feared for his country, it was because he saw its moral character being ravaged by a decadent luxury. "Plain living and high thinking are no more."[3] In September, 1802, when England was living through some of the gravest days of its history, the poet pleaded with his country to find its salvation in virtue. He longed for a Milton to "raise us up, return to us again; And give us manners, virtue, freedom, power." Like the Romans looking back upon Cato, Scipio, Scaevola, Wordsworth recalled the "Moralists" who once gave England power—Marvell, Sidney, Harrington.[4] Clearly Wordsworth believed that the only triumph England could hope to win was a moral one. And he stuck to this principle. In 1816 his hymns of victory were hymns to England's "Magnanimity," which had so gloriously defeated the unbridled passions of France.[5]

Wordsworth's two sonnets, "On a Celebrated Event in Ancient History," prove that, like the Romans, he believed liberty dependent upon the virtue of a people. At the Isthmian Games in 196 B.C. Titus Flamininus proclaimed in the name of the Roman Empire that

2. *Excursion,* VIII, 214–30. Cicero in his *Tusc Disp* (v, xxiii) describes the "buried tomb" of Archimedes. Plutarch in his life of Marcellus (p. 262) says: "But he esteeming all kind of handicraft and invention to make Engines, and generally all manner of Sciences bringing common commodity by the use of them, to be but vile, beggery, and mercenary dross: employed his wit and study only to write things, the beauty and subtilty whereof, were not mingled any thing at all with necessity." See also Livy, xxv, xxiv, 11–14; xxv, xxxi, 9–10. Cicero, *De Finibus,* v, xix, 50. For other lines showing Wordsworth's sympathy for the figure of Archimedes, see *Prelude,* XI, 435.
3. "O Friend! I know not which way I must look."
4. "Great men have been among us; hands that penned."
5. "Hail, orient Conqueror of gloomy Night!"

Greece should once again enjoy her ancient liberty. The proclamation was received with wild acclaim by all the assembled Greeks.

> . . . birds, high flying in the element,
> Dropped to the earth, astonished at the sound!

According to Wordsworth only the Ætolians were wise enough to see that true liberty can never be bestowed as a gift upon the conquered, the "feeble spirits." Whether the year be 196 B.C. or 1809 A.D., one principle holds fast: "A nation, without the virtues necessary for the attainment of independence, have failed to attain it."[6]

These two sonnets are a rare instance of Wordsworth's direct use of Roman history. In the detail of picture and narrative the first sonnet follows exactly Plutarch's account.[7] But the judgments which Wordsworth made on the event could hardly have been suggested by Plutarch. Plutarch would never have allowed the Ætolians the epithet of "thoughtful"; according to him they were unjustly envious and certainly not able judges of the moral law. The only hint of possible sympathy of judgment between Wordsworth and Plutarch occurs in the comparison of Philopoemen with Titus Quintius Flamininus: ". . . they do well, that do commend *Titus* Acts, for his clemency and courtesie used to the GRECIANS: but much more the Noble and Valiant Acts of *Philopoemen* unto the ROMANS. For it is much easier to pleasure and gratifie the weak, then it is to hurt and resist the strong."[8] Nor, as might be expected, is there much similarity of opinion between Wordsworth and Polybius. Polybius himself was so thoroughly involved in the event that he could not help being influenced by a natural patriotism for the Achaeans.[9] It is in Livy that we find the closest approximation to Wordsworth's judgment, and strangely enough it is in a speech of Lycortas, the father of Polybius![1] His defense of the Greeks and the reply of Appius Claudius give support to Wordsworth's analysis of a liberty bestowed upon a people by an outside sovereignty.[2]

---

6. *Prose Works*, I, 51 ("The Convention of Cintra").
7. Plutarch, pp. 320 ff. (Flaminius [sic]).   8. *Idem*, p. 329.
9. For Polybius' utter scorn for the Ætolians, see Polybius, pp. 182–3; 461–2. For Polybius' political activity in Greece see Wilhelm Schmid and Otto Stählin, *Geschichte der Griechischen Literatur*, Vol. II, No. 1, pp. 384–5. (Iwan von Müller, *Handbuch der Klassischen Altertums-Wissenschaft* [Munich, 1920].

1. Livy, XXXIX, xxxvi, 6 to xxxvii, 18. (Polybius summarizes this speech in Book XXIV [see Polybius, *The Histories*, with an English translation by W. R. Paton (Loeb Classical Library), v, 437 ff.] but the fragment is not found in Grimeston's translation.) Livy himself, like the other historians, thought that the "liberty" granted the Greeks was a supreme gift, another example of Rome's magnanimous spirit (*idem*, XXXIII, xxxii–xxxiii), and he too felt little admiration for the Ætolians (*idem*, XXXIII, xi, 4–10). The speech which Livy does allow an Ætolian is not sufficiently reflective to have mattered to Wordsworth (*idem*, xxxiv, xxiii, 5 ff.).

2. Cf. Jakob A. O. Larsen, "Was Greece Free between 196 and 146 B.C.?" *Classical Philology*, XXX (July, 1935), 193–209.

The independence which marks Wordsworth's treatment of the "celebrated event" is characteristic. He did not use the Romans for the sake of poetic translations; rather, he so absorbed their philosophy that he was able to attack their *opinions* with their own *principles*. They believed that liberty belonged as a natural right to the virtuous and to no others, but in this particular case the classic historians were either so much impressed with Rome's magnanimity that they misused their own philosophy[3] or they imagined the Greeks good men and, therefore, possessed of a natural right.[4]

As Wordsworth accepted the Roman doctrine that national security and liberty depend upon national virtue, so too he accepted the Roman views on international affairs. Most Roman writers believed that war could best be justified on moral grounds. In his attempt to glorify Rome Livy took particular pains to discover moral justification for Rome's frequent wars.[5] Because this view has been so long held by all reasonable men it cannot be regarded as strictly Roman in character, and certainly Wordsworth's insistence upon moral justification for war cannot be credited to the Romans. But several of his comments are worth observing because they show him using Roman history to justify his own point of view. In 1811 he wrote to Captain Pasley that, "The spirit of conquest, and the ambition of the sword, never can confer true glory and happiness upon a nation that has attained power sufficient to protect itself."[6] He then proved his point by referring to the irrevocable sin committed by the Romans in undertaking their famous defense of the Mamertines. According to Wordsworth the Romans' decision to wage war outside Italy led them to forsake their old morality and eventually brought upon them all the sins and misfortunes of civil war at home.[7]

Wordsworth's criticism of the Romans who began the First Punic War shows him familiar with the debates that preceded Rome's entry into Sicily. Undoubtedly his chief source was Polybius.[8] He agreed with Polybius that the action was unjust; that the Romans had reason to fear the Carthaginians but that they were most winningly persuaded by the hope of plunder.

That Wordsworth deplored the Roman seizure of foreign lands does not mean that he condemned all Roman history after the subjugation of Italy. Like Tacitus, he saw examples of nobility in later

3. Plutarch, pp. 321-2.
4. Livy, xxxiv, xlix, 11. (Flamininus' parting advice to the Greeks: "Alienis armis partam, externa fide redditam libertatem sua cura custodirent servarentque, ut populus Romanus dignis datam libertatem ac munus suum bene positum sciret.")
5. Livy, vii, xxxi; ix, viii ff.; xxi, xviii–xix; xxxvii, liv, 14–16, 28.
6. *MY*, I, 437. 7. *Ibid*.
8. See Polybius, pp. 6–7. Wordsworth was reading Polybius the same month he wrote to Captain Pasley; see *MY*, 1, 443. In Livy he could find nothing except the *Periocha* of Book XVI.

Rome: "Non tamen adeo virtutum sterile saeculum ut non et bona exempla prodiderit."[9] But he did give his unqualified allegiance to early Rome.[1] In this he was not alone. As we have already observed, the classic historian had looked back upon the early Republic as the Golden Age of Rome, and often he had regretted the price that was paid for the Empire's final supremacy.

It was common for the historians to connect the decadence of late Rome with the downfall of its foreign enemies. After Rome's enemies were overcome, the people missed the necessary discipline of fear, and the love of country gave way to love of power and money.[2] When Wordsworth adopted the same philosophy for the sake of his own country, I believe we are justified in concluding that he drew directly upon the Romans. In the letter to Captain Pasley, he argued for a balance of power in Europe: his reasons would have astonished most nineteenth-century statesmen. He desired that England should feel the pressure of foreign powers—because fear would make the people virtuous. ("From needing danger, to be good . . . Lord deliver us.")

Of course, Wordsworth's trust in virtue as the only source of national salvation is the more surely proved by his having adopted such a remarkable theory of international relations. He must, indeed, have been very sincere in the belief that virtue should be the chief political principle, if he were willing to invite the harshest discipline possible that might secure it. Moreover, the fact that he was here so distinctly Roman argues well for a Roman influence wherever he connected morality and national well-being. The passage deserves to be quoted, at least in part; the references to Scipio are probably drawn either from Florus, whom Wordsworth quotes elsewhere in the letter, or from Plutarch's life of Cato.[3]

I wish to see Spain, Italy, France, Germany, formed into independent nations; nor have I any desire to reduce the power of France further than may be necessary for that end. Woe be to that country whose military power is irresistible! I deprecate such an event for Great Britain scarcely less than for any other Land. Scipio foresaw the evils with which Rome would be visited when no Carthage should be in existence for her to con-

---

9. *Hist.*, I, 3.
1. See *LY*, I, 364 (March 3, 1829). This letter is an example of Wordsworth's sticking to principles at the same time that he changes his opinion on the application of principles; in 1829 he commends the conquests of Rome, particularly the early ones, because he now thinks they were "moral."
2. Sallust, *Bell Jug*, XLI, 1–5; Sallust, *Bell Cat*, X, 1–6; Tacitus, *Hist.*, II, 38; Florus, I, xlvii ("Cuius aetatis superiores centum anni sancti, pii et, ut diximus, aurei, sine flagitio, sine scelere, dum sincera adhuc et innoxia pastoriae illius sectae integritas, dumque Poenorum hostium inminens metus disciplinam veterem continebat . . . nescio an satius fuerit populo Romano Sicilia et Africa contento fuisse, aut his etiam ipsis carere dominanti in Italia sua, quam eo magnitudinis crescere, ut viribus suis conficeretur. Quae enim res alia civiles furores peperit quam nimiae felicitates?").
3. Florus, I, xxxi; Plutarch, p. 301 (Marcus Cato).

tend with. If a nation have nothing to oppose or to fear without, it cannot escape decay and concussion within. Universal triumph and absolute security soon betray a State into abandonment of that discipline, civil and military, by which its victories were secured.[4]

If it is accepted that Wordsworth entrusted both national and international welfare to a principle of virtue, the question may well be asked, what sort of virtue did he look for? Were nations to be ruled, as in Plato's *Republic*, by the virtuous wisdom of philosopher statesmen? Or was the ruling virtue to be a more strictly political virtue, as in Aristotle's *Politics*, a virtue "relative to the constitution"?[5] I believe that the answer is neither. The virtue to which Wordsworth entrusted the welfare of his state was merely a composite of the simple, homely virtues, neither philosophical nor political. Moreover, these virtues were not limited to any special class of society, but rather were spread throughout the whole nation. Certainly Wordsworth's praise for "The old domestic morals of the land"[6] was very much in the Roman fashion. It is difficult to say whether or not he was ever conscious of this similarity to the Romans; I think he sometimes was.

> ... and over all
> *A healthy sound simplicity should reign,*
> *A seemly plainness, name it what you will,*
> *Republican or pious.*[7]

When the Augustan writers praised the men of early Rome they emphasized always their simplicity, frugality, modesty, *pietas*—in a word, the *republican* manners. Livy perhaps more than any other prose writer glorified the Republic for the sake of its virtuous men.[8] Beside him stand the poets, Vergil and Horace. We must not forget that Horace wrote often of the republicans—Fabricius, Camillus, Cato—and that he too selected their modest virtues for particular praise.[9] It may well be that the Roman influence apparent in Wordsworth's views on the domestic virtues is principally Horatian.[1] But,

---

4. *MY*, I, 438. See also Wordsworth on the effect in England of Napoleon's defeat, *Prose Works*, I, 229 ("Two Addresses").
5. Aristotle, *Politics*, III, 1276 b, Benjamin Jowett, tr. (Oxford, 1908).
6. *Excursion*, VIII, 236.
7. *Prelude*, III, 398–401. (Italics are mine.)
8. Livy, IV, vi, 11–12; V, xlix–liv; VII, i, 8–10; VII, xl, 2.
9. Horace, *Odes*, I, xii, 37–44; II, xv; III, vi, 33–44. (*The Odes and Epodes*, with an English translation by C. E. Bennett [Loeb Classical Library].)
1. In her analysis of the Horatian influence on Wordsworth, Miss Mary Rebecca Thayer does not emphasize this particular aspect, but her general conclusion is here pertinent: "we find Wordsworth the most Horatian of all the poets considered in this study." (*The Influence of Horace on the Chief English Poets of the Nineteenth Century* [New Haven, 1916], p. 32.) Her study includes Coleridge, Byron, Shelley, Keats, Tennyson, and Browning.

so far as he connected any particular domestic virtues to the general welfare of his country, he is closest to the prose writers.

Let us take for example the virtue of frugality. Many classic writers praised this domestic virtue for its salutary effect upon the state.[2] The rhetoric of Livy almost persuades us that Cincinnatus was a successful dictator mainly because he worked his own four-acre farm;[3] in Plutarch we find the illustrious deeds of national heroes enhanced and even partly explained by the poverty of their estates.[4] The introduction of eastern luxury—the *Persicos apparatus* which Horace so hated—had for the Romans a historical significance.[5] To combat the evils of luxury, to recover the virtues of frugality, became a serious occupation of later statesmen.[6]

It is unlikely that the spirit of frugality which Wordsworth celebrates in such a poem as "Michael" has any direct connection with the Romans. But Wordsworth was convinced that the homely virtues of Michael were vital to the state. In 1801 he addressed a letter to Fox, recommending to his attention those poems of 1800 which describe the conditions of England's small landowners: he concluded that for the good of the state the *frugal*, industrious farmer must be preserved.[7]

Because Wordsworth found his virtuous men scattered throughout the country and because he believed these men to be the source of England's strength, it followed logically that he could never accept the "romantic" doctrine of hero and hero worship. Like the Romans, he was ready to praise the noble dead and, like them, he felt that the very name of his country was hallowed by the heroic men who had fought for its freedom. Much of the success of Cicero's Second Verrine Oration hangs upon the significance he was able to discover in that simple sentence—"Civis Romanus sum."[8] In Livy one of the most stirring orations is that of Camillus persuading the people to rebuild their city; he succeeds by appealing to the citizens that they be worthy of their heroic ancestry.[9] So, too, Wordsworth:

> . . . In our halls is hung
> Armoury of the invincible Knights of old:
> We must be free or die, who speak the tongue
> That Shakespeare spake; the faith and morals hold
> Which Milton held.—In every thing we are sprung
> Of Earth's first blood, have titles manifold.[1]

2. Cicero, *Tusc Disp*, III, viii, 16–18; Tacitus, *Ann*, II, 33; Tacitus, *Hist.*, II, 38; Livy, XXXIV, i and iv; Plutarch, pp. 33–49 (Lycurgus, *passim*).
3. Livy, III, xxvi, 7–12. See also Livy on the estate of Agrippa, II, xxxiii, 10.
4. Plutarch, p. 221 (Paulus Æmylius).   5. Livy, XXXIX, vi, 7–9.
6. See, for example, Tacitus, *Ann*, III, 52–5.   7. *EL*, pp. 259–63.
8. *In C. Verrem*, II, v, 62, §162 ff., in *The Verrine Orations*, L. H. G. Greenwood, ed. and tr. (Loeb Classical Library, 1928–35, 2 vols.).   9. Livy, v, xlix–liv.
1. "It is not to be thought of that the Flood." Cf. also Polybius, pp. 80–1.

But such praise of dead heroes is clearly not after the *romantic* school of hero worshippers. Indeed, some of Wordsworth's most vigorous attacks are directed against the false elevation of a single man.[2] He chose not to attach the name of Nelson to "The Character of the Happy Warrior," and on the death of England's hero he quoted instead an old ballad:

> I trust I have within my realm
> Five hundred good as he.[3]

This is the spirit of Gaius Mucius in the camp of Porsenna,[4] or of the Spartan woman silencing the praise of her dead son: "*Brasidas* was indeed a valiant man, but the Country of LACONIA hath many more yet valianter then he was."[5]

Roman writers did not consider the possibility of hero worship in the *romantic* sense of the word. They recognized no perfect, unchanging hero,[6] and they filled their histories with the rise and fall of one man after another.[7] It was no wonder that a man schooled in Plutarch, and hence familiar with the Greek practice of ostracism, should have condemned all forms of hero worship as "pernicious and degrading."[8] Wordsworth's reading in Roman prose may well have helped to convince him that "a man's past services are no sufficient security for his future character; he who to-day merits the civic wreath may to-morrow deserve the Tarpeian rock."[9] Furthermore, whenever he did celebrate contemporary figures, they were martyrs to liberty, men such as Tacitus' Agricola who had succeeded not through power but through virtue, and even these were chosen as representative of principles active in all men.[1]

So far I have been concerned only with Wordsworth's political principles and their relation to Roman prose. In describing principles fundamental to his political thought, I have drawn at random from the works of Wordsworth. Such a procedure has been possible because from beginning to end the *principles* remained the same. But

2. Isabella Fenwick note to "At Vallombrosa" (*Prose Works*, III, 92).
3. *MY*, I, 6.
4. Livy, II, xii, 8-11.
5. Plutarch, p. 46 (Lycurgus).
6. Plutarch, p. 410: "the meer frailty of mans nature . . . cannot bring forth a man of such vertue and perfection, but there is ever some imperfection in him" (Cimon).
7. Plutarch, *passim*; Nepos, *passim*; Livy on the trial of the Scipios, XXXVIII.
8. Isabella Fenwick note to "Hail, orient Conqueror of gloomy Night!" (*Prose Works*, III, 75.)
9. *Prose Works*, I, 18 ("Apology for the French Revolution").
1. See Wordsworth's note to "The King of Sweden" and also *MY*, II, 711.

it is equally clear that his views on the application of those principles changed considerably over a period of years, and that another kind of procedure—a strictly chronological one—is now necessary.

The peculiar character of Wordsworth's politics, which allowed him to subscribe to the same principles even as his practices underwent radical changes, has been well described by John Stuart Mill in a letter to John Sterling, October 22, 1831:

> . . . he [Wordsworth] talks on no subject more instructively than on states of society and forms of government . . . The next thing that struck me was the extreme comprehensiveness and philosophic spirit which is in him . . . Wordsworth seems always to know the pros and the cons of every question; and when you think he strikes the balance wrong it is only because you think he estimates erroneously some matter of fact . . . you have only to discuss with him the "how much," the more or less of weight which is to be attached to a certain cause or effect as compared with others: thus the difference with him turns upon a question of varying or fluctuating quantities . . . and the whole question is one of observation and testimony, and of the value of particular articles of evidence. I need hardly say to you that if one's own conclusions and his were at variance on every question which a minister or a Parliament could to-morrow be called upon to solve, his is nevertheless the mind with which one would be really in communion; our principles would be the same, and we should be like two travellers pursuing the same course on the opposite banks of a river.[2]

Mill does not explain why Wordsworth came to estimate "erroneously some matter of fact," why he crossed from one bank to another, and certainly it is not within the province of this study to attempt an explanation. But in order to understand the various uses to which he put his political principles we must consider his changing views on society, views which incidentally help to explain his so-called political "apostasy."

When Wordsworth first became wholeheartedly interested in political movements, he looked upon society in general as more like than different and more good than bad.[3] In *The Prelude* he recalled that, when he first "began To meditate with ardour on the rule And management of nations," he was prepared mainly by a faith in the goodness of human nature.[4]

---

2. *The Letters of John Stuart Mill*, Hugh S. R. Elliot, ed. (London, 1910, 2 vols.) I, 10–11. Quoted by Edith C. Batho, *op. cit.*, pp. 13–15.

3. *EL*, p. 262: He hopes that his poems "may in some small degree enlarge our feelings of reverence for our species, and our knowledge of human nature, by shewing that our best qualities are possessed by men whom we are too apt to consider, not with reference to the points in which they resemble us, but to those in which they manifestly differ from us." *Prose Works*, I, 163–4 ("The Convention of Cintra").

4. *Prelude*, XI, 98–100.

> I had approached, like other youths, the shield
> Of human nature from the golden side,
> And would have fought, even to the death, to at
> The quality of the metal which I saw.[5]

Even his stay in London had contributed to this view. There his *historical* sense of what had been done and suffered in that great city effected "still more elevated views Of human nature."[6]

> Add also, that among the multitudes
> Of that huge city, oftentimes was seen
> Affectingly set forth, more than elsewhere
> Is possible, the unity of man,
> One spirit over ignorance and vice
> Predominant, in good and evil hearts;
> One sense for moral judgments, as one eye
> For the sun's light.[7]

Another passage of *The Prelude* (XIII, 217–20), in which Wordsworth insisted on the fundamental likeness and goodness of all men, has drawn an interesting comment from Professor Havens: "In emphasizing the constant factor in human experience, in regarding all men as basically much the same, Wordsworth is in the classic tradition. It is the romanticist who stresses individual uniqueness, the unusual in character or experience, local color, transitory aspects of nature."[8] In a sense this is a true criticism. If Professor Havens uses the term "classic tradition" to mean the tradition originally established by the Greeks and Romans, he can easily find support. We have only to think of Cicero's memorable words: "Nihil est enim unum uni tam simile, tam par, quam omnes inter nosmet ipsos sumus."[9] Of course, it is only *potentially* that we are all much alike; *actually* some men are good and others are bad, and the philosopher-statesman observes carefully that fact when he discusses civil laws.[1]

The early Wordsworth made little distinction between the potentially good society of man and that which actually exists. Right or wrong, he constantly merged the two and, as we shall see, he then proceeded to apply his principles of politics with a lavish, democratic hand. The spirit of youthful idealism suggests that the early Wordsworth found greater satisfaction in the dictums of Rousseau on the goodness of natural man than in the detached, philosophical arguments of the classicists.[2]

---

5. *Idem*, XI, 79–82. 6. *Idem*, VIII, 644–5. 7. *Idem*, VIII [665–72].
8. Havens, *The Mind of a Poet*, p. 595. 9. Cicero, *De Legibus*, I, x, 29.
1. See, for example, Cicero on the plebeian tribunate, *De Legibus*, III, x.
2. Godwin too believed in the fundamental likeness of all men: "'the points in which human beings resemble are infinitely more considerable than those in which they differ.'" Quoted by Harper, I, 259.

As Wordsworth's views on society underwent gradual modification, as he came more and more to find virtuous men limited in number, he naturally—even logically and consistently—modified the application of his general principles. What was once good for all society later became good for only a portion of society. It is difficult to find in Wordsworth's later poetry expressions of his revised opinions on society, partly, perhaps, because his imagination needed a more expansive and exalted subject.[3]

Although most of the expressions of his early faith occur in *The Prelude*, they are there described in retrospect, and for that reason the same poem offers examples of two points of view. At the end of *The Prelude* the poet set out to find the virtuous men who constitute a nation's wealth, mournfully inquiring at the same time why "this glorious creature [is] to be found One only in ten thousand."[4] Wordsworth's revisions of *The Prelude* provide us with other indications of his growing disbelief in the goodness of total society. About 1804 he described his early hope for the exertions of a good leader in revolutionary France; he based that hope on the fact that,

> A Spirit thoroughly faithful to itself,
> Unquenchable, unsleeping, undismay'd,
> Was as an instinct among Men.[5]

Sometime before 1820 these lines were revised:

> A spirit thoroughly faithful to itself,
> Is for Society's unreasoning herd
> A domineering instinct.[6]

In *The Excursion* Wordsworth was careful to show that much of the Solitary's despair followed inevitably upon an unnatural confidence in the good of human society.[7] By 1818 Wordsworth's distrust included even the good people of Westmorland. In that year the letters of the Wordsworths, particularly Dorothy's, were filled with scorn for the blue-ribboned ragamuffins, the mobs, the rabble, the disaffected. The chief premise of the "Two Addresses" was that society left to itself would foist its own evils upon the nation.

Wordsworth's later views on society were more thoroughly in accord with those of the classic writers, at least with those of the political and historical writers of Rome, than were his earlier ones. Many

---

3. See Wordsworth (January, 1824) on the imagination, *LY*, I, 134–5.
4. *Prelude*, XIII, 87–8.
5. *Idem*, x (A-text), 148–50. For date, see De Selincourt, *Prelude*, pp. xxxix–xl.
6. *Prelude*, x, 167–9. MS. C gives revised reading (see variant reading, p. 370) and MS. C was copied sometime between 1813 and 1820, probably about 1817–19 (see De Selincourt, *Prelude*, p. xviii).
7. *Excursion*, IV, 260 ff.

classic authors spent their force in attacks upon the "unreasoning herd."[8] Always Livy's most complete scorn is directed against men who abase themselves before the mob.[9] The mob of Shakespeare's *Julius Caesar* is fairly representative of the common people as they are pictured in Rome's histories.

To understand Wordsworth's use of the same political principles in totally different ways, it is helpful to observe for whom the principles were to operate. If we keep in mind his early faith in the goodness of total society, his arguments for a democratic form of government become understandable. In the same way, if we remember his later disillusionment, we can understand better his arguments for a hierarchical republic. A survey of Wordsworth's application of political principles to specific problems must, therefore, be a chronological one; because Wordsworth usually treated specific problems only in prose, the survey may be a brief one.

Although Wordsworth spoke of himself in 1794 as a member "of that odious class of men called democrats,"[1] he did not observe the classic distinction between a democracy and a republic. In his "Apology for the French Revolution" (1793) he came out strongly in favor of a republic which should express the general will of the people. Because the virtues were all that mattered, no economic qualification should limit the political power of the people.[2] Of course, Wordsworth was never so blind as to imagine that Utopias would spring up all over Europe once the virtuous many came into their own, but he did envisage a steady and sure improvement in a government of the people, by the people, and for the people.[3] Because the Romans shared no such faith in the virtue of the common people, they had supported a representative form of government in which the power of different groups was checked and balanced by the power of other groups.[4] In Wordsworth's earliest formal political statement he differed, therefore, from the Romans in his application of a fundamental principle.

Curiously enough it was in his attitude toward economic reforms that Wordsworth came closest to the Romans.[5] In the "Apology" he protested that he was "not an advocate for the agrarian law nor for sumptuary regulations";[6] but the mere fact that he used a terminology peculiar to Rome argues a certain connection. He believed that no

---

8. Livy, XXIV, XXV, 8–9; XXXI. xxxiv, 3; XLII, xxx, 1. Tacitus, *Hist.*, III, 83; IV, 38.
9. See, for example, Livy on Appius Claudius, III, xxxv.
1. *EL*, pp. 115–16.   2. *Prose Works*, I, 11.   3. *Idem*, I, 10–11.
4. Polybius, pp. 288–92; Cicero, *De Legibus*, III, v, 12 ff. Cicero's *De Re Publica*, which most clearly argues for a government of checks and balances (I, xlv–xlvi), has not been used in this study because Wordsworth could not have read it until after 1822 at the earliest.
5. His specific references to the Romans are merely rhetorical. See *Prose Works*, I, 20.
6. *Idem*, I, 16.

true political liberty could exist together with great economic inequality.[7] His vague generalizations for reform suggest that he had attended more carefully to the French interpretation of antique legislation than to the studies of contemporary economists.[8]

Sixteen years later, in his most ambitious work on contemporary politics, Wordsworth continued to support a republican form of government. In his tract on the Convention of Cintra he expressed the hope that Spain might enjoy under a republic the large portion of civil liberty which she so well deserved. He found that Spain had been best governed when its national power was administered through small, provincial assemblies.[9] The Supreme Junta to which she had been forced to yield was too far removed from the people, and a "pernicious Oligarchy" had resulted.[1] Wordsworth would have preferred to have had the power revert to the Cortes because it was more representative of the nation as a whole.

The reasons for Wordsworth's faith in the possibility of a republic in Spain show him applying strictly a principle of Roman political philosophy. The Spanish people were morally fit for civil liberty as the French had not been. "Spain has nothing to dread from Jacobinism. Manufactures and Commerce have there in far less degree than elsewhere . . . enfeebled their bodies, inflamed their passions by intemperance, vitiated from childhood their moral affections, and destroyed their imaginations."[2] The character of Madrid made it a potential Rome; Paris had shown itself to be little more than an unhappy Capua.

In 1816, four years after Spain had drawn up her first liberal constitution, Wordsworth changed his mind. At first sight it might appear that he had repudiated his own principles. He had hoped for a representative government in Spain; finally it had arrived, and he hastened to condemn it. But it is clear that the same principle motivated Wordsworth in 1816 as in 1809. Once he had thought Spain morally capable of civil liberty; later he discovered that the Cortes was composed of men "not equal to that task."[3] Without repudiating the benefits of representative government, Wordsworth came to the unhappy conclusion that nations can enjoy only "that portion of civil Liberty which their ignorance and vices permit them to enjoy."[4]

The "Two Addresses" ought not to come as a shock to readers of Wordsworth's letters. A growing disbelief in the goodness of society

7. *Idem*, I, 15–16.
8. The French made much of Plutarch's accounts of the life and works of Tiberius and Caius Gracchus, both of whom had expressed revolutionary doctrine on the power of the tribune (see Plutarch, p. 687); and of Solon's legislation for economic reform in Athens (see Plutarch, pp. 72, 93).
9. *Prose Works*, I, 146.
1. *Idem*, I, 147.   2. *Idem*, I, 161.   3. *MY*, II, 712.   4. *Idem*, II, 751.

is reflected in Wordsworth's writing from at least 1814 onward; a love of hierarchy,[5] of "enlightened subordination,"[6] of general stability become more and more prominent. In 1814 to secure "gradation of power," he invoked the example of Rome and showed himself at least a practical historian, if not a practical statesman.

Every one knows of what importance the equestrian order was in preserving tranquillity and a balance and gradation of power in ancient Rome; the like may take place among ourselves through the medium of an armed yeomanry; and surely a preservative of this kind is largely called for by the tendencies of things at present.[7]

What is shocking in the "Two Addresses" is the discovery that for Wordsworth men of property had now become the men of virtue. In some ways one might wish that he had forsaken his moral principles and had taken a new political stand based on economic principles alone. It is small comfort to recall that long before he had made excellent poetry on the love of landed property, one of "the most powerful affections of the human heart."[8] The fact remains that, because he found love of landed property tending to raise the moral standard, property became in the end the final test of a man's integrity[9] and, therefore, the imperative qualification both for election and for suffrage. Since he sincerely believed that virtue was most active in the propertied class, he did stick to his principles in entrusting to men of property the affairs of the state.

Wordsworth's distrust of the "petty Artizans, Shop-keepers, and Pothouse Keepers"[1] may be more easily tolerated if it is remembered that he believed these men, given political power, would lose England her liberty. To Wordsworth of the eighteen-twenties and -thirties Reform meant extending political power to men morally incapable of sustaining liberty, men destined to succumb before immoral despotism.[2] After that the whole battle for liberty would have to be fought again.

In 1818 Wordsworth was more nearly Roman than was Camillus Gracchus Babeuf of 1794. He had got beyond the revolutionary dreams of Rome, beyond the aping of mere forms, to a similar political philosophy. By 1818 he was supporting a government of checks and

---

5. *LY*, I, 358.
6. Wordsworth's note to "Hail, orient Conqueror of gloomy Night!"
7. *MY*, II, 585.
8. See Wordsworth's criticism of "Michael" in a letter to Thomas Poole, *EL*, p. 266. In Wordsworth's early views on property there is often a suggestion of Plutarch. Cf. Plutarch, p. 59: "For there is no exercise nor occupation in the world which so suddenly bringeth a man to love and desire quietness, as doth husbandry and tillage, and yet to defend a mans own, there is in it courage and hardiness to fight" (Numa).
9. *Prose Works*, I, 240. For the moral effects of property see *idem*, I, 251–2; *LY*, I, 321.
1. *Prose Works*, I, 244.   2. *Idem*, I, 250; *LY*, II, 704, 723.

balances out of fear that political power in the hands of the people would end in the establishment of tyranny.[3]

It is not out of a desire to ingratiate Wordsworth with modern political philosophy that I conclude by remarking upon his consistent opposition to all forms of tyranny. Such a conclusion is merely a convenient way to show Wordsworth's lifelong attachment to Roman history. At the beginning of the French Revolution he had been inspired by the thoughts of ancient heroes who had opposed the tyrannies of their own day. In words reminiscent of Cicero, he recalled the ancient truths, known to philsophers, known to Brutus,

> . . . that tyrannic power is weak,
> Hath neither gratitude, nor faith, nor love,
> Nor the support of good or evil men
> To trust in; that the godhead which is ours
> Can never utterly be charmed or stilled;
> That nothing hath a natural right to last
> But equity and reason; that all else
> Meets foes irreconcilable, and at best
> Lives only by variety of disease.[4]

As he approached the end of his own battles against tyranny, he returned to Plutarch and wrote the well-known poem on Dion.

Dion was a figure peculiarly attractive to both Plutarch and Wordsworth; he was a man of magnanimous virtues, a man valiant in the defense of the liberties that rightly belonged to his countrymen. The historic incidents, even the tone and imagery, of Plutarch's narrative are all repeated in Wordsworth. Both writers linger over passages descriptive of Plato's teaching of Dion and the rewarding effects of that teaching revealed in the character of the hero.[5] Both writers are quickened by the excitement and glory of Dion's triumphant entry into Syracuse.[6] In the poem there is, of course, much that is omitted. For example, Wordsworth omits the story of Dion's second banishment, brought upon him by the countrymen whom he had saved, his patience and long-suffering in exile, and his hard-won fight for a new Sicilian liberty. Wordsworth's omissions make for differences between the two historical accounts, but they are, after all, unimportant differences. Somewhat more important is the difference in Wordsworth's treatment of the vision that appeared to Dion. Wordsworth makes a connection between the vision and Dion's own remorseful sense of guilt; Plutarch, on the other hand, thinks of the vision as something sent to foreshadow what is to come rather than to comment on what is past.

3. Cf. Polybius, pp. 286–7.
4. *Prelude*, x, 200–08. Cf. Cicero, *De Officiis*, II, vii, 23.
5. Plutarch, pp. 799–803.   6. *Idem*, p. 807.

The truly significant difference comes in Wordsworth's interpretation of the cause leading to Dion's final failure. According to Wordsworth, Dion points a universal truth:

> 'Him, only him, the shield of Jove defends,
> Whose means are fair and spotless as his ends.'[7]

Murder was a means that Dion once employed. In the published version of the poem, Wordsworth spoke of the murder in rather vague, general terms. Dion, he tell us,

> Hath stained the robes of civil power with blood,
> Unjustly shed, though for the public good.[8]

In a manuscript revision of the poem, Wordsworth expanded this section and, without confuting the moral of the poem, yet managed to emphasize the wickedness of Dion's victim. He whom Dion unjustly killed was, according to Wordsworth, a man "Ambitious fickle envious turbulent."

> Untractable disturber of the state,
> Repeated pardons make him more elate
> And bolder to transgress again;
> He hath provoked his fate.[9]

In Plutarch it is quite a different story, one which by its very difference illustrates the aristocratic sympathies of the later Wordsworth. Heraclides accused Dion of denying the people their right to govern themselves. Plutarch, partial as he is to Dion, yet admits the justice of that charge.

Indeed to confess a troth, *Dion* had sent for certain CORINTHIANS, hoping the better to establish the form of a Commonwealth, which he had in his mind when they were come. For his mind was utterly to break the government of *Democratia* . . . and to establish the LACONIAN or CRETAN Commonwealth, mingled with a princely and popular Government: and that should be, *Aristocratia* . . . And for that purpose he thought the CORINTHIANS the meetest men to help him to frame this Commonwealth, considering that they governed their affairs more by chusing a few number of the nobility, then otherwise; and that they did not refer many things to the voice of the people. And because he was assured that *Heraclides* would be against him in it all he could, and that otherwise he knew he was seditious, a troublesome, and light headed fellow: he then suffered them to kill him . . .[1]

---

7. "Dion," Lines 123–4.   8. Lines 56–7.
9. MS. variant to ll. 57–9 in *The Poetical Works of William Wordsworth*, E. De Selincourt, ed. (Oxford, 1944), p. 275. For date of MS., see *idem*, p. 520.
1. Plutarch, p. 815.

When a real conspiracy later developed, Dion was unwilling to take action against it, for he had come to look upon the murder of Heraclides as a "foul blot."[2] Rather than suffer more suspicion and doubt, he welcomed his own death.

It is not too much to suppose that, had Wordsworth written his poem a few years earlier, the reason assigned the hero's failure would have had a different interpretation. Surely, the early Wordsworth could ill have brooked the aristocratic turn to Dion's politics. But the point to be emphasized here is the constancy of Wordsworth's underlying principles. So long as Dion acted justly to secure Sicilian liberty, the desired end was assured; but a single failure in virtue entailed a loss of liberty. And so we are brought back to that fundamental political principle shared by the Romans and by Wordsworth: the salvation of a state depends wholly upon the virtue operative in that state.

The tract on the Convention of Cintra, written seven years previously, proves that this principle motivated Wordsworth's practical politics. Dion had failed to bring the people of Syracuse a lasting liberty because he had failed to observe the only successful means. So too, by one means only, could England aid the Spanish and defeat a new tyranny. "Our duty is—our aim ought to be—to employ the true means of liberty and virtue for the ends of liberty and virtue."[3]

2. *Idem*, p. 816.   3. *Prose Works*, I, 136.

III

Wordsworth and Roman Stoicism

IN describing certain aspects of Wordsworth's poetry, modern critics frequently use the adjective "stoical."[1] Sometimes the adjective is used in a popular sense to denote merely the natural austerity of character which his poetry reflects. Sometimes it is used to define more precisely ideas of Wordsworth's which are comparable to those of the ancient Stoics. But in either case the adjective "stoical" is used only for the sake of illustration and interpretation. No attempt is made to relate directly Wordsworth's stoicism to the classical philosophy of that name.

Among modern critics Professor Beatty alone thinks it "almost certain" that Wordsworth's stoicism is in a direct line of descent from the ancient Stoics.[2] But the comments of Professor Beatty, illuminating as they are, are unfortunately limited to brief notes in his edition of Wordsworth's *Representative Poems*. There is, therefore, no thorough study of Wordsworth's stoicism in its relation to the classic philosophy.

Such a study should form a part of this larger work on Wordsworth's reading of Roman prose. It should do so because the Stoics whom Wordsworth read were Roman writers. In Wordsworth's time the fragments of the Greek Stoics were hard to come by; whatever he knew of the early Stoics must have been derived from the Romans. Unfortunately the records of his library give us few hints of his reading in Roman philosophy. We know only that his library contained the works of Cicero, as well as several copies of *De Officiis*[3] (Wordsworth always speaks of Cicero as the "philosophic" Cicero); a copy of the *Manual* of Epictetus, printed with a Latin translation facing the original Greek;[4] another copy of Epictetus—whether the *Discourses* or the *Manual* is unknown;[5] and a copy of Diogenes Laertius, the Greek text being accompanied by a Latin translation.[6]

1. See, for example, A. C. Bradley, *Oxford Lectures on Poetry* (London, 1934), p. 118; William Ralph Inge, *Studies of English Mystics* (London, 1907), p. 178; Newton P. Stallknecht, "Wordsworth's *Ode to Duty* and the Schöne Seele," *PMLA*, LII (1937), 230–7; Newton P. Stallknecht, *Strange Seas of Thought* (Durham, 1945), pp. 25–6; E. A. Sonnenschein, "Stoicism in English Literature," *The Contemporary Review*, CXXIV (1923), 355–65.
2. Arthur Beatty, ed., *Wordsworth: Representative Poems*, p. 626, n. 2.
3. See above, p. 13.   4. *Rydal Mount*, Lot 409.
5. Harvard University MS., p. 2 ("Catalogue of Wordsworth's Library in the Hand of His Daughter").   6. *Rydal Mount*, Lot 111.

In this chapter my aim is threefold: first, to present evidence for Wordsworth's knowledge of Roman Stoicism; secondly, to show how closely Wordsworth approximated the total philosophy of the Stoics; thirdly, to discover to what extent and with what effects Wordsworth's ethical philosophy was influenced by his reading in Roman Stoicism.

The classical learning of any well-read man represents a knowledge not only of the Greeks and Romans but also of the traditions established by them. It is for this reason impossible to parcel out Wordsworth's knowledge of Roman Stoicism and label each piece with the name of a Roman. For example, it is known that Wordsworth read closely the works of Francis Bacon,[7] and it is known too that the works of Bacon are copiously illustrated with quotations from the Roman Stoics.[8] The same is true of Montaigne; it is a rare essay that draws nothing from Seneca.[9] Professor Beatty has remarked on Wordsworth's early reading of Bolingbroke and reminded us that Bolingbroke too had a marked fondness for Seneca.[1] Wordsworth himself has drawn attention to the use of Seneca made by one of his favorite English poets, Samuel Daniel.

Daniel is a particularly interesting example because of Wordsworth's specific reference. In the fourth book of *The Excursion* Wordsworth describes in Stoic terms the wise who, unperturbed by any adversity, enjoy always a perfect liberty of mind. Eight lines of this description consist of a direct quotation from Daniel's epistle "To the Lady Margaret, Countesse of Cumberland." In a note attached to the passage Wordsworth observes that the last two lines of the quotation are a translation from Seneca.

*'And that unless above himself he can
Erect himself, how poor a thing is Man!'*[2]

7. See *EL*, p. 559. *MY*, I, 233, 297–8; II, 748. "Essay Supplementary to the Preface" (*The Poetical Works*, Hutchinson, ed., p. 946): "But that his [Shakespeare's] Works . . . made but little impression upon the ruling Intellects of the time, may be inferred from the fact that Lord Bacon, in his multifarious writings, nowhere either quotes or alludes to him."

8. Richard Mott Gummere, *Seneca and His Modern Message* (Boston, 1922), pp. 114–16.

9. Camilla Hill Hay, *Montaigne, lecteur et imitateur de Sénèque* (Poitiers, 1938). For Wordsworth's copies of Montaigne, see *Rydal Mount*, Lots 51, 357.

1. Beatty, *op. cit.*, pp. 626–7, n. 2.

2. *Excursion*, IV, 330–1. In his note to these lines Wordsworth quotes four stanzas from Daniel's epistle; he includes the whole poem in his *Poems and Extracts Chosen . . . for an Album . . . Christmas, 1819* (London, 1905), pp. 84–91; he gives it particular praise in a letter to Sir George Beaumont (*MY*, II, 477). Coleridge has spoken of the remarkable likeness between Daniel and Wordsworth (*Biographia Literaria*, J. Shawcross, ed. [Oxford, 1907, 2 vols.], II, 119). For specific connections between the poetry of Daniel and Wordsworth, see *MY*, I, 198–9, and Helen Darbishire, ed., *Wordsworth: Poems in Two Volumes, 1807* (Oxford, 1914), pp. 364, 453.

These lines are a translation from Seneca's *Naturales Quaestiones*;[3] so far as I have been able to discover, Wordsworth was the first to identify the translation. That he was able to do so suggests that his knowledge of Seneca was as wide as it was thorough. As a general rule the *Naturales Quaestiones* are less frequently quoted or referred to than are the *Epistles* and *Dialogues*.

Wordsworth's reference to Seneca's *Naturales Quaestiones* was made in the first edition of *The Excursion*, 1814. As a motto for his "Ode to Duty," composed in 1804, Wordsworth adapted a quotation from the *Moral Epistles*.[4] A study of Wordsworth's poems composed between 1804 and 1814 reveals a wealth of pure Stoic philosophy expressed in language frankly reminiscent of the Latin writers. From these poems it becomes apparent that, when in *The Excursion* he wrote specifically of Stoicism,[5] he was basing his critical remarks on a solid knowledge.

In a review of Stoicism as it was known to Wordsworth, we are forced to deal with a philosophy that developed and changed over hundreds of years. Between Cicero and Marcus Aurelius many original minds left their marks upon this philosophy, and many others incorporated into the philosophy ideas drawn from Plato, the New Academy, and even Epicurus.[6] For this reason exceptions could be made to many of the general statements by which I attempt to summarize Roman Stoicism. In view of this difficulty it may be well to list the chief sources upon which my statements are based: Cicero, *De Natura Deorum, Academica, De Finibus Bonorum et Malorum, De Officiis, Tusculanae Disputationes;* Seneca, *Dialogi, De Clementia, De Beneficiis, Epistulae Morales, Naturales Quaestiones;* Epictetus, *Manual, Discourses;* Marcus Aurelius, *Meditations;* Diogenes Laertius, life of Zeno in *Lives and Opinions of Eminent Philosophers*. Since Wordsworth probably knew Cicero and Seneca best, preference has been given to them.

Because Stoicism is a whole philosophy, it ought to be viewed with a sweep of the eye.[7] But, since that is impossible to all but the very wise, it has been conveniently divided into three parts—one dealing with nature, another with reason, and another with ethics.[8] These parts are all highly integrated; a problem in ethics is explained by

3. I, Praef 5: "O quam contempta res est homo, nisi supra humana surrexerit!"
4. *Ep*, cxx, 10: "iam non consilio bonus, sed more eo perductus, ut non tantum recte facere posset." The motto does not appear until the 1836–37 edition of *The Poetical Works of William Wordsworth* (London, 6 vols.), v, 46–8.
5. *Excursion*, III, 330–66.
6. For the history of Stoicism, see E. Vernon Arnold, *Roman Stoicism* (Cambridge, 1911); Eduard Zeller, "Die Philosophie der Griechen," Dritter Teil, Erste Abteilung, *Die Nacharistotelische Philosophie*, Erste Hälfte (Vierte Auflage, Leipzig, 1909).
7. Seneca, *Ep*, LXXXIX, 1.
8. Seneca, *Ep*, LXXXIX, 2, 9; LXXXVIII, 24. Diogenes Laertius, p. 460 [VII, xxxiii].

reference to metaphysics, a problem in metaphysics is explained by reference to logic, and so forth. Because the character of each part is understood in relation to the whole, the unity of Stoic philosophy requires us to consider all three parts.

It is for this reason that the Stoic *ethics,* which alone directly concerned Wordsworth, cannot be studied singly as an independent branch of the total philosophy. But the need to discuss, however briefly, the whole nature of Stoicism is not without a distinct advantage. The fact that Wordsworth's philosophy, informal as it is, corresponds closely to the whole philosophy of the Stoics justifies and partly explains his adoption of Stoic ethics. He was drawn to the Stoics because they taught a philosophy like his own. He was justified in adopting portions of their philosophy because each portion could be perfectly integrated with his own total philosophy. For example, Wordsworth, like the Stoics, recognized a cosmic order; he could, therefore, adopt that portion of Stoic ethics which teaches the value of bringing the individual will into harmony with the general order of things. Obviously here is a case where, without a similar view on the nature of the universe, Wordsworth could not take over the *ethical* teaching of Stoicism.

Stoicism is essentially a monistic philosophy, for according to all Stoics there is only one ultimate reality. All that exists is body. The Stoical argument that supports this fundamental doctrine is a simple one: everything capable of acting or being acted upon is body; everything that exists either acts or is acted upon; therefore, everything that exists is body.[9] Despite the seemingly dual nature of body, the Stoics are careful to preserve their monistic system. The fact that body is either active or passive does not entail two separate realities, for the primary body out of which everything is created contains within its single unified self both active *and* passive principles.[1]

In Stoic philosophy the active principle is identified wth the Logos, or God. Since the active principle is inseparable from body, God is likewise inseparable from body. The passive principle is regularly regarded as matter without quality, while the active is Reason, or God within body.[2] But both the active and the passive, both matter and God, are of a single unified body: they may be distinguished only as mental concepts.[3] Marcus Aurelius exults in the contemplation of this Oneness:

---

9. Cicero, *Acad,* I, xi, 39. See Zeller, *op. cit.,* p. 119.
1. Diogenes Laertius, p. 519 [VII, lxviii]. See Zeller, *op. cit.,* p. 134: "So entschieden daher die Körperlichkeit alles Wirklichen von den Stoikern behauptet wird, so unterscheiden sie doch innerhalb des Körperlichen selbst wieder zwei Prinzipien: das Leidende und das Wirkende, den Stoff und die Kraft."
2. Diogenes Laertius, p. 519 [vii, lxviii].
3. Arnold, *op. cit.,* pp. 172-3.

Even consider and thinke upon the world, as being but one living substance, and having but one soule, and how all things in the world, are terminated, into one sensitive power . . . and are done by one generall motion as it were, & deliberation [*of that one soule;*]and how all things that are, concurre in the cause of one anothers being, and by what manner of connexion and concatenation all things happen.[4]

Since body is all that there is, body is the first cause and "creates" only in the sense that it acts upon itself to effect changes in its form. In other words, God, or the active principle, acts upon matter, or the passive principle, to give to body a different aspect. The processes of all change, therefore, present God moving through matter. "Nempe universa ex materia et ex deo constant. Deus ista temperat, quae circumfusa rectorem secuntur et ducem."[5] The universe in its present state and in its future conflagrations is created by God, and as such it is everywhere filled with God acting upon matter. The Stoics were keenly aware of the presence of God, or the active principle, filling the whole matter of the universe. To say "God is immanent in nature" meant to a Stoic more than can easily be conceived of today when this phrase has been dulled by use in all kinds of modified philosophies of nature. Something of its Stoic meaning may come through to us when we think of a few of the qualities characteristic of nature, or the universe.

First, the universe is rational. The proof of this attribute is to be found in one of the paradoxes of Zeno: " 'Quod ratione utitur id melius est quam id quod ratione non utitur; nihil autem mundo melius; ratione igitur mundus utitur.' "[6] This syllogism is the model for many others. In the same way the universe is proved to be good, wise, happy, eternal, etc. Another argument proves that the world is sentient: there cannot be a sentient part of an insentient whole; part of the world is sentient; therefore, the whole is sentient.[7] The qualities so deduced are evidence that there exists nothing better than the world. God, therefore, who is best, is the world and possesses all the attributes of the world—He is rational, sentient, good, beautiful, etc.[8]

Another way to approach the Stoic idea of God's immanence is to observe particular examples. It is comparatively easy to accept the metaphysical doctrine that God as the active principle is everywhere; the notion of "body," as God acting through matter, somehow means more to an unphilosophical mind when it is observed in concrete terms.

---

4. *Meditations*, IV, xxxiii. Square brackets are translator's. See also *idem*, VI, xxxiv.
5. Seneca, *Ep*, LXV, 23. See also Seneca, *De Beneficiis*, IV, viii, 2; "opus suum ipse inplet."
6. Cicero, *Nat Deo*, II, viii, 21.   7. *Idem*, II, viii, 22.
8. *Idem*, II, viii, 21: "Ex quo efficietur esse mundum deum."

Quocumque te flexeris, ibi illum videbis occurrentem tibi; nihil ab illo vacat, opus suum ipse inplet. Ergo nihil agis, ingratissime mortalium, qui te negas deo debere, sed naturae, quia nec natura sine deo est nec deus sine natura, sed idem est utrumque, distat officio.[9]

Quid est deus? Mens universi. Quid est deus? Quod vides totum et quod non vides totum. Sic demum magnitudo illi sua redditur, qua nihil maius cogitari potest, si solus est omnia, si opus suum et intra et extra tenet.[1]

prope est a te deus, tecum est, intus est . . . sacer intra nos spiritus sedet.[2]

ordo autem siderum et in omni aeternitate constantia neque naturam significat (est enim plena rationis) neque fortunam quae amica varietati constantiam respuit; sequitur ergo ut ipsa sua sponte suo sensu ac divinitate moveantur.[3]

These statements inevitably raise the question, is Stoicism a pantheistic philosophy? If pantheism means that God is everything, Stoicism is *not* pantheistic. God, as the active principle, is an aspect of body, and body, it is true, is everything. God is body, but everything is not God. Matter, the passive principle, is not God, although it too is body. Two aspects of one thing are not the same. Critics of Wordsworth's philosophy have used a term which is equally appropriate to Stoicism—"panentheism."[4] In a panentheistic philosophy God moves through matter but is not matter.

The distinction was a clear one to all Stoics. The early Stoics usually thought of God as fire: the vital warmth, the creative heat in all nature. To think of fire as ether was natural to the ancient physicists; God, therefore, could become the fiery spirit, or simply the spirit and soul of all created matter.[5] He is thus spoken of by most of the Roman Stoics. "Quem in hoc mundo locum deus obtinet, hunc in homine animus."[6]

Because God provides the creative impulse, or, more properly, sets in motion changes in body, the Stoics necessarily looked upon the universe as a cosmos. Everything that happens, every change that occurs, is ordered. The government of the universe is directed by God. When God is regarded as first cause, the chain of causes (*nexio causarum*) is often termed "Fate."[7] When the first cause is regarded as God in the sense of personal deity, the chain of causes is termed

---

9. Seneca, *De Beneficiis*, IV, viii, 2.   1. Seneca, *NQ*, I, Praef. 13.
2. Seneca, *Ep*, XLI, 1–2. See also Epictetus, *Discourses*, II, viii, 2.
3. Cicero, *Nat Deo*, II, xvi, 43.
4. Inge, *op. cit.*, p. 179; A. D. Martin, *The Religion of Wordsworth* (London, 1936), p. 14. Arnold, *op. cit.*, p. 219, defends Stoicism against charges of pantheism. But see Zeller, *op. cit.*, p. 149.
5. Zeller, *op. cit.*, pp. 141–4.   6. Seneca, *Ep*, LXV, 24.
7. *Idem*, XVI, 4–5; XCIII, 1–2. Cicero, *Nat Deo*, I, xv, 39.

"Providence."[8] The only difference apparent is one of attitude; the Stoic who thinks of God in more personal terms usually speaks of Providence.[9]

The fact that God governs the universe inevitably makes for a good universe. "Whatever is, is right." Whether the Stoic uses the term Providence or the term Fate makes no difference; he finds all good.[1] This view of a determinist world is especially important to ethics, and it shall be discussed later in our study of Stoic ethics.

Selected passages from Wordsworth's poetry might well have been used to describe the natural philosophy of Roman Stoicism. Almost every aspect of the philosophy which has here been described is somewhere described better by Wordsworth. Because this is so, I am confronted with the danger of inadvertently suggesting some kind of influence. But no reason exists for supposing that Stoic *metaphysics* exerted a formative influence upon Wordsworth. In fact, there are several reasons for supposing that it did not. For one, Wordsworth devoted much of his most convincing poetry to those unique experiences out of which he drew his ideas on the nature of things. It was surely not in a philosophical disquisition on the "vital force,"[2] but rather in a "serene and blessed mood," peculiar to himself, that Wordsworth saw "into the life of things." Besides, if anyone wanted to find a formal source for Wordsworth's metaphysics, Spinoza would do quite as well as the Stoics; perhaps even better, for Wordsworth heard Coleridge talk about Spinoza in 1797,[3] and apparently his own serious reading in Stoicism did not begin until about 1804. Much of his natural philosophy which corresponds to the Stoic philosophy was written before 1804. It is not, therefore, with the idea of suggesting Stoicism as an influence that fundamental likenesses are here observed: it is simply that, without a total philosophy similar to that of the Stoics, Wordsworth could not have adopted the *ethical* teaching of Stoicism.

Although Wordsworth's philosophy suffered many changes in form and expression, certain basic principles were rarely, if ever, repudiated. The revisions in *The Prelude* show him attempting to make his early philosophy consonant with his later religious faith; but there was no attempt to throw everything overboard and take on something quite different and contradictory. In a summary which aims only at discovering the likenesses between Wordsworth's philosophy

---

8. Seneca, *Dial*, I ("De Providentia"), *passim*; Cicero, *Nat Deo*, II, xxx, 75 ff.
9. Arnold, *op. cit.*, pp. 202–03.   1. Seneca, *Ep*, LXXIV, 20.
2. See, for example, Cicero, *Nat Deo*, II, ix–xi.
3. See S. T. Coleridge, *Biographia Literaria*, I, 127. Professor Melvin M. Rader remarks upon the essential likenesses between Wordsworth's natural philosophy and that of Spinoza (*Presiding Ideas in Wordsworth's Poetry*, University of Washington Publications in Language and Literature, November, 1931, p. 203, n. 22).

and that of the Stoics, the shifts in tone and emphasis may be ignored.

Like the Stoics, Wordsworth held a monistic philosophy. He believed that a "mighty unity" embraces all that is.[4] A "false secondary power" of the mind creates division and prevents our recognizing "The unity of all,"[5] "the mighty whole" in which we all exist.[6] Unlike the Stoics, Wordsworth did not give this unity a name. "Body" would have been for him connotative of modern materialistic philosophies; on the other hand, "spirit" would not have been sufficiently inclusive. Had Wordsworth used a metaphysical terminology, he would probably have chosen something like the ὄν of the early Stoics.

He was able to get along without a precise definition because he concentrated upon one aspect of this unity rather than upon the unity in its entirety. For Wordsworth a life principle distinguished the oneness in which all things are, and it was to this principle that he devoted his attention. Early and late he was conscious of the one continuous life,[7] which animates "this active universe"[8] and gives to everything "a vital pulse."[9] His own most lively moments sprang from his consciousness of life everywhere:

> . . . I was only then
> Contented, when with bliss ineffable
> I felt the sentiment of Being spread
> O'er all that moves and all that seemeth still;
> O'er all that, lost beyond the reach of thought
> And human knowledge, to the human eye
> Invisible, yet liveth to the heart;
> O'er all that leaps and runs, and shouts and sings,
> Or beats the gladsome air; o'er all that glides
> Beneath the wave, yea, in the wave itself,
> And mighty depth of waters.[1]

Dean Inge has, I think, rightly characterized Wordsworth's sense of life as essentially Stoical: "Not the sense of beauty, but of eternal and ubiquitous *life*—of an universe animated throughout, and obeying one law—this thought, which is rather Stoical than Platonic, is most prominent in Wordsworth."[2]

As the Stoics identified the active principle with God, so Wordsworth recognized that "the one Surpassing Life . . . is And hath the name of God."[3] In his early poetry the terms God and life are often interchangeable—so unregarded was the notion of either a personal

---

4. *Prelude*, xiii (A-text), 254–5.   5. *Idem*, ii, 215–21.
6. Lines from a MS. notebook, printed in De Selincourt, *Prelude*, p. 512.
7. *Excursion*, iv, 755.   8. *Prelude*, ii, 254; see also xi (A-text), 147.
9. *Idem*, viii, 480.
1. *Idem*, ii, 399–409; see also iii, 130–5.
2. Inge, *op. cit.*, p. 178.
3. *Prelude*, vi (A-text), 154–7.

or transcendent deity.[4] It is not that Wordsworth denied the transcendence of God, but rather that he affirmed the presence of God *in* His works.[5] As the active principle, the animating force in the universe, God is necessarily present in everything. For this reason Wordsworth conceived the process of creation in much the same way as did the Stoics. The presence of God in matter gives movement and life to matter, provides the vitality of everything. In times of heightened consciousness Wordsworth actually recognized in the things around him a power which is "like workings of one mind,"[6] and which he identified with the creative force of God.

> And I have felt
> A presence that disturbs me with the joy
> Of elevated thoughts; a sense sublime
> Of something far more deeply interfused,
> Whose dwelling is the light of setting suns,
> And the round ocean and the living air,
> And the blue sky, and in the mind of man:
> A motion and a spirit, that impels
> All thinking things, all objects of all thought,
> And rolls through all things.[7]

Since the mind of God is diffused through all nature, the mind of man necessarily participates in the divine mind[8] and thus enjoys a creative power of its own.[9] In contemplating the divinity of man, Wordsworth makes his most daring statement:

> —In which all beings live with god, themselves
> Are god, Existing in the mighty whole,
> As indistinguishable as the cloudless East
> At noon is from the cloudless west, when all
> The hemisphere is one cerulean blue.[1]

Such statements are defended against the charges of pantheism much as the Stoics are defended against pantheism: although God exists

---

4. Havens, *The Mind of a Poet,* chap. ix, pp. 179–200.
5. *Prelude,* x (A-text), 386–9. See also *MY,* II, 618: The author of *The Excursion* "does not indeed consider the Supreme Being as bearing the same relation to the Universe, as a watch-maker bears to a watch."
6. *Prelude,* VI, 636.
7. "Lines Composed a Few Miles Above Tintern Abbey," ll. 93–102. C. C. Bushnell, *The Journal of Germanic Philology,* IV (1902), 58, compares these lines with Lucan's *De Bello Civili,* IX, 578–80: "Estque dei sedes, nisi terra et pontus et aer/et caelum, et virtus? . . . Iuppiter est, quodcumque vides, quodcumque moveris." It should be noted that Lucan is the Stoics' poet. For Wordsworth's copies of Lucan, see *Rydal Mount,* Lots 397, 531.
8. *Prelude,* v (A-text), 10–17.
9. *Idem,* II, 255–60; "Lines Composed a Few Miles Above Tintern Abbey," ll. 105–07.
1. Lines from a MS. notebook printed in De Selincourt, *Prelude,* pp. 512–13.

in nature, He is not specifically limited to nature, and as an indwelling power He is distinguished from that in which He dwells.[2]

His belief in the immanence of God led Wordsworth to other conclusions similar to those of the Stoics. First, the universe is a cosmos ordered by God. The divinity of natural law preserves "the stars from wrong,"[3] and the same divinity purposefully directs the fate of men. God by His very nature converts everything to good; this universe is as good as it is active.[4] In the passage from *The Excursion* to which I have referred, an objection might be raised that Wordsworth there speaks of a personal benevolent deity. But even in passages where the immanent God is thought of simply as the life principle, Wordsworth reached the same conclusion.

> 'Tis Nature's law
> That none, the meanest of created things,
> Of forms created the most vile and brute,
> The dullest or most noxious, should exist
> Divorced from good—a spirit and pulse of good,
> A life and soul, to every mode of being
> Inseparably linked.[5]

To make a summary of Wordsworth's metaphysical ideas is to repeat all that has been said of Stoic metaphysics. Wordsworth and the Stoics both believed that the ultimate reality was a unity embracing everything that is. Both conceived this unity as possessing an active principle, which may be identified with God. As the active principle in the universe, God orders the life of everything and, therefore, makes all things good. In its essential features Wordsworth's philosophy parallels that of the Stoics. Although it is quite unlikely that Stoicism had any influence upon the formation of his natural philosophy, I think that, in at least one passage of his later poetry, Stoicism did perhaps suggest certain philosophical terms. The ninth book of *The Excursion* was written after Wordsworth had acquired a knowledge of Roman Stoicism. The vocabulary which he there used to express ideas independently arrived at long before is remarkably Stoic.

> To every Form of being is assigned,
> . . . .
> An *active* Principle:—howe'er removed
> From sense and observation, it subsists

---

2. Rader, *op. cit.*, p. 180. Cf. Inge, *op. cit.*, pp. 175–82; Havens, *op. cit.*, pp. 187–8.
3. "Ode to Duty," l. 47. Cf. "Gipsies," ll. 23–4 ("Life which the very stars reprove As on their silent tasks they move") and Seneca, *Ep*, xc, 42, "sidera superlabebantur et insigne spectaculum noctium mundus in praeceps agebatur silentio tantum opus ducens."
4. *Excursion*, IV, 14–17. Cf. Seneca, *Ep*, LXXIV, 20.
5. "The Old Cumberland Beggar," ll. 73–9.

> In all things, in all natures; in the stars
> Of azure heaven, the unenduring clouds,
> In flower and tree, in every pebbly stone
> That paves the brooks, the stationary rocks,
> The moving waters, and the invisible air.
>
> . . . .
>
> Spirit that knows no insulated spot,
> No chasm, no solitude; from link to link
> It circulates, the Soul of all the worlds.
> This is the freedom of the universe;
> Unfolded still the more, more visible,
> The more we know; and yet is reverenced least,
> And least respected in the human Mind,
> Its most apparent home.[6]

The "active Principle" (*principatus*), the "Soul of all the worlds" (*animus universi*), the movement from "link to link" (*vinculum circumdatum*) are terms employed by Stoic philosophers. From Cicero's *De Natura Deorum* alone could come countless examples.

Natura est . . . quae contineat mundum omnem . . . et ea quidem non sine sensu atque ratione; omnem enim naturam necesse est quae non solitaria sit neque simplex sed cum alio iuncta atque conexa habere aliquem in se principatum, ut in homine mentem, in belua quiddam simile mentis unde oriantur rerum adpetitus; in arborum autem et earum rerum quae gignuntur e terra radicibus inesse principatus putatur. Principatum autem id dico . . . quo nihil in quoque genere nec potest nec debet esse praestantius; ita necesse est illud etiam in quo sit totius naturae principatus esse omnium optimum omniumque rerum potestate dominatuque dignissimum.[7]

Omne igitur quod vivit, sive animal sive terra editum, id vivit propter inclusum in eo calorem. Ex quo intellegi debet eam caloris naturam vim habere in se vitalem per omnem mundum pertinentem.[8]

Maxime autem corpora inter se iuncta permanent cum quasi quodam vinculo circumdato colligantur; quod facit ea natura quae per omnem mundum omnia mente et ratione conficiens funditur.[9]

That part of the Stoic philosophy which deals with problems of knowledge can be briefly described, for, although it is essential to the total philosophy, it was treated with comparative brevity by the

---

6. *Excursion*, IX, 1–20. Stallknecht argues that Wordsworth was here influenced by Shaftesbury and Boehme (*Strange Seas of Thought*, pp. 130–7). His argument is based almost entirely upon internal evidence (see *idem*, pp. 71–2), and does not, I think, invalidate my point.

7. Cicero, *Nat Deo*, II, xi, 29.   8. *Idem*, II, ix, 24.   9. *Idem*, II, xlv, 115.

Romans themselves. In a discussion of logic, the Romans usually began by establishing the basic principle that knowledge is attainable. They established this principle in two ways: first, by refuting the scepticism of the Academics[1] and, secondly, by analyzing the ways in which knowledge *is* acquired. Since the first method contributes little to Stoicism as a whole, it may here be omitted. The second method, however, brings us to the heart of the matter.

According to the Stoics, knowledge begins with sense perception. But, even at this first stage in the process of learning, the mind is not passive; from beginning to end the Stoics recognize the voluntary activity of the mind.[2] At the level of sense perception, the mind "grasps" the thing presented (*visum*) to the senses. The grasp of the thing presented, or the voluntary assent given to sensation, is true knowledge—if the *visum* is clear (obviously manifest) and if the assent cannot be shaken by reasoning.[3]

Sense perceptions are stored in the mind and are there compared one with another. By a process of analogy the *visa* so stored are eventually united into "notions."[4] These "notions" are mental concepts, and as true knowledge they too must receive the active assent of the mind. Since the "notions" spring from a combination of *visa*, they are also based ultimately upon the senses.

But, in making judgments upon the thing perceived, the Stoic employs certain preconceptions, which derive not from the senses but from the mind. For example, all men have a preconception of certain qualities—such as sweetness and bitterness; when objects, sweet or bitter, are presented to the senses, the judgment made by all men is derived from their common sense.[5] Preconceptions, therefore, constitute a form of knowledge which is stimulated by the senses but is derived from the mind.

Other more advanced forms of knowledge are derived from the mind alone. These have to do with ideas of God, of what is morally good, etc., and as innate ideas they too exist in all men. Evidence of innate ideas is found in the fact that men agree on certain questions, and it is for this reason that Stoics make much of the common consent of mankind: "Multum dare solemus praesumptioni omnium hominum, et apud nos veritatis argumentum est aliquid omnibus videri. Tamquam deos esse inter alia hoc colligimus, quod omnibus insita de dis opinio est nec ulla gens usquam est adeo extra leges moresque proiecta, ut non aliquos deos credat."[6] The divinity of man is proved by the fact that his innate ideas are shared by God, or, to put it the

---

1. Cicero, *Acad*, II, vi, 17 ff.
2. Arnold, *op. cit.*, p. 137.
3. Cicero, *Acad*, I, xi, 39–41.
4. *Idem*, II, x, 30; Seneca, *Ep*, cxx, 4 ff.
5. Cicero, *Acad*, II, vii, 21.
6. Seneca, *Ep*, cxvii, 6. See also Cicero, *Tusc Disp*, I, xiii, 30; Cicero, *Nat Deo*, II, iv, 12: "omnibus enim innatum est et in animo quasi insculptum esse deos."

other way around, the innate ideas possessed by man are a part of the divine mind.[7] As such, of course, the mind of man is creative, for, as we have already observed in our study of Stoic metaphysics, creation is achieved through the activity of God, or Logos.[8] Among the later Stoics, Seneca is the one most given to emphasizing the divinity of the human mind; he attacks all forms of sophistry, what Wordsworth calls "false secondary powers" that set up "puny boundaries."[9] His attitude on questions of knowledge explains much of his attraction for Wordsworth.

Compared with the Stoics, Wordsworth is without a systematic philosophy of knowledge. Except for the period during which he adopted in part Hartley's theory of association, Wordsworth made no attempt to explain the whys and wherefores of simple learning. When we remember that he distrusted analytic reasoning, much as did Seneca, his failure to analyze the nature of logic is understandable. But, wherever he spoke of knowledge, of the senses, and of reason, he approximated the main tenets of Stoic logic.

For one thing, Wordsworth believed that the senses provide accurate knowledge. How they do so, he did not explain, but his confidence that the external world is "exquisitely" fitted to the individual mind indicates a confidence in the truth of sense perception.[1] Like the Stoics he also believed that the mind of man possesses certain innate ideas.[2] Wordsworth held that man possesses these innate ideas by virtue of the divinity of the human mind. Here we see an example of how one part of philosophy plays into another. The natural philosophies of both Wordsworth and the Stoics taught the immanence of God; from this teaching it necessarily followed that the mind of man participates in the mind of God.[3]

In pursuing the implications of a belief in transcendental knowledge, Wordsworth reached conclusions similar to those of the Stoics. First, the senses are subservient to the mind. Wordsworth had no terminology correspondent to the Stoic "assent" but he thought of the acceptance of sense perceptions as being an act of will.

---

7. Cicero, *Nat Deo*, II, xxxi, 79. Epictetus, *Discourses*, III, iii. Seneca, *Ep*, XCII, 1; LXVI, 12: "Ratio autem nihil aliud est quam in corpus humanum pars divini spiritus mersa."
8. Seneca, *Ep*, LXV, 2.
9. Seneca, *De Beneficiis*, VI, i, 1. Seneca, *Ep*, XLV, *passim;* LXXXIX, 3; LXXXVIII, *passim;* CXI, *passim*.
1. "Prospectus," preface to *The Excursion*, ll. 66-8.
2. See Rader, *op. cit.*, chap. iii, pp. 147-59.
3. *Prelude*, v (A-text), 10-17; XIV, 448-54. *Excursion*, IV, 50-1: "By thy grace The particle divine remained unquenched." Sonnenschein, *op. cit.*, p. 364, notes that Wordsworth's "'particle divine' reproduces the Stoic imagery (*divinae particula aurae*, Horace, *Sat.* ii, 2, 79)." Casaubon in his translation of Marcus Aurelius makes the same translation: Marcus Aurelius knows "that this transgressor, whosoever he be, is my kinsman, not by the same blood and seed, but by participation of the same reason, and of the same *divine particle*." (*Meditations*, I, xv. Italics are translator's.)

> This efficacious spirit chiefly lurks
> Among those passages of life that give
> Profoundest knowledge to what point, and how,
> The mind is lord and master—outward sense
> The obedient servant of her will.[4]

Another conclusion based upon his faith in innate ideas was that the common consent of mankind is evidence of true knowledge. He found the common consent implicit in the religions of Persia, Babylon, Chaldea, Greece, evidence for the existence of a "higher reason and a purer will,"[5] and in his most optimistic moments he entrusted to the common consent of men judgments on moral issues.[6] A third conclusion is that the mind of man, sharing divinity with God, enjoys a creative power of its own. In developing this idea Wordsworth reached a whole new conception of the imagination and its functions and went far beyond anything in Stoic logic. For the purposes of this study it is sufficient merely to point to the fundamental likeness between the *active* nature of Wordsworth's imagination and the *active* nature of the Stoic mind. Both are imitative of the divine mind.

> For feeling has to him imparted power
> That through the growing faculties of sense
> Doth like an agent of the one great Mind
> Create, creator and receiver both,
> Working but in alliance with the works
> Which it beholds.[7]

Mens enim ipsa, quae sensuum fons est atque etiam ipsa sensus est, naturalem vim habet quam intendit ad ea quibus movetur.[8]

The monistic character of Stoic philosophy makes it inevitable that one part of the philosophy should repeat the thought of the other two parts. From different points of view the teacher of physics, the teacher of logic, and the teacher of ethics all looked at the same thing.[9] The repetition that resulted is at once the glory of the philosophy and the bane of such a study as this. We move in circles and summarize the same thing three times.

This state of affairs becomes immediately apparent when it is ob-

---

4. *Prelude*, XII, 219–23.   5. *Excursion*, IV, 666–762.   6. *Prelude*, VIII [671–72].
7. *Idem*, II, 255–60; see also XIII (A-text), 68–90.
8. Cicero, *Acad*, II, x, 30. See also Seneca, *Ep*, LXV, 2–3: "Materia iacet iners, res ad omnia parata, cessatura, si nemo moveat. Causa autem, id est ratio, materiam format et quocumque vult versat, ex illa varia opera producit . . . Omnis ars naturae imitatio est."
9. Cicero, *De Finibus*, III, x, 33: "eorum [Stoicorum] definitiones paulum oppido inter se differunt, et tamen eodem spectant."

served that to the Stoics man is a microcosm. All that has been said of the universe may be said of man alone. His body and soul are held together in a unity; he rules himself by reason; he shares reason with God, life or soul (*anima*) with the animals, and a growing nature with plants.[1] In the same way the study of ethics repeats the study of logic. The activity of the mind reflects an act of will, and, therefore, good logic is equivalent to good ethics. ("Virtus non aliud quam recta ratio est. Omnes virtutes rationes sunt.")[2] Since by implication much of the ethics has already been described, and since details concerning the ethics will naturally accumulate in the Wordsworth criticism that follows, a summary is here all that is necessary.

According to the Stoics the good is virtue—they are confident that nothing better than virtue can be conceived of and they delight in refuting arguments that propose other goods such as knowledge or pleasure.[3] All ethics, of course, is directed to the good, and, in the case of the Stoics, virtue is the whole aim of ethics.

The Stoics define virtue as living according to nature.[4] What this means becomes clear when we discover that every thing has *by nature* a ruling principle.[5] Virtue, therefore, consists in maintaining the ruling principle in the order which nature intended. In man the ruling principle is reason, his "particle" of God.[6] In fulfilling the nature of reason, man can be said to portray God.[7]

Since reason is not developed in the child, the child does not possess virtue. In the child action is directed by instinct. The behavior of the child shows an instinct for self-preservation; his acts, therefore, are "appropriate" acts in that they tend to preserve his nature.[8] The difference between the "appropriate" acts of the child and the "virtuous" acts of the wise man is the difference between action based on instinct and action based on principle.[9] The wise man exerts his reason to discover what is best for his nature; in the exercise of that reason he has already attained virtue.[10]

Since man is a part of the universe, what is best for the universe is also best for man.[11] In seeking to discover the laws of his own nature,

1. Arnold, *op. cit.*, p. 242.   2. Seneca, *Ep*, LXVI, 32.
3. Cicero, *Tusc Disp*, v, xvi, 48; Cicero, *Acad*, I, x, 35.
4. Seneca, *Dial*, VII ("De Vita Beata"), viii, 2; Seneca, *Ep*, CXXIV, 14; Cicero, *De Finibus*, III, vi, 20-2.
5. Cicero, *Nat Deo*, II, xi, 29.
6. Seneca, *Ep*, CXXIV, 23; XCII, 1-2. Cicero, *Tusc Disp*, v, xxv, 70.
7. Seneca, *Dial*, VII ("De Vita Beata"), xvi, 1.
8. Cicero, *De Finibus*, III, v, 16; III, vi, 20.
9. *Idem*, III, xviii, 59.
10. Virtue for the Stoic is complete once the intention to act is formulated; the success of the action can add nothing to the absolute virtue formulated by reason. See *idem*, III, ix, 32; Seneca, *De Beneficiis*, II, xxxi, 1.
11. Marcus Aurelius, *Meditations*, I, xvii; IV, xix; v, viii; v, xix. Epictetus, *Discourses*, II, v, 4; II, x, 1.

man must learn the laws of universal nature. Again we are brought back to the Stoic physics. As we have already observed, the universe is a cosmos ordered by God, or Logos, and as such the universe is good. In ethics, therefore, man is taught to live willingly in accordance with the laws of the universe. In his willingness lies all his freedom.[3]

In their praise of reason all Stoics praise the same means to the same end: the exercise of reason will lead men to a life according to nature. But different Stoics choose different examples to illustrate the single theme, and as a result their writings show superficial differences—differences mainly of emphasis and temperament. A description of these differences is the easiest way to learn the various *functions* of virtue.

In general, Cicero has his Stoic speakers consider virtue in the humbler spheres of practical life. Among other things he shows that the four cardinal virtues, justice, courage, temperance, and prudence, are aspects of the single virtue[4] (that is, life according to nature); that the virtuous man observes specific duties to family, friends, and state;[5] that the expedient is the same as the good (for whatever is good is expedient);[6] that some things are to be valued, some rejected, and some regarded indifferently.[7] The impression that one gets from the Stoic writing of Cicero is the practical good sense of life according to nature.

Seneca, on the other hand, writes of virtue in a more exalted way. As he describes the functions of virtue, we are conscious of two striking characteristics. First, by the exercise of reason the wise man may return to that divine source from which he took his nature.[8] In the contemplation of this end Seneca gave to his writings a quality which was later particularly admired by the early Christians.

... patria est illi quodcumque suprema et universa circuitu suo cingit, hoc omne convexum, intra quod iacent maria cum terris, intra quod aer humanis divina secernens etiam coniungit, in quo disposita tot lumina in actus suos excubant.[9]

Sed 'Si cui virtus animusque in corpore praesens,' hic deos aequat, illo tendit originis suae memor. Nemo inprobe eo conatur ascendere, unde descenderat . . . Et si [animus] utatur suis viribus ac se in spatium suum extendat, non aliena via ad summa nititur.[1]

---

3. Epictetus, *Manual*, 2, 13. Epictetus, *Discourses*, I, xii, 2; II, xvi, 4; IV, i, 14. Marcus Aurelius, *Meditations*, II, vi; IV, xxviii.
4. Cicero, *De Officiis*, I, xxvii, 100. Cicero, *De Finibus*, III, 7, 24.
5. Cicero, *De Officiis*, II, xxi, 73; III, x, 43; I, xvii, 58.
6. *Idem*, III, iii, 11 ff.   7. Cicero, *De Finibus*, III, vi, 20; III, xv, 50.
8. Seneca, *Ep*, XLI, 5; LXXIII, 16; CXX, 13–5. Seneca, *NQ*, I, Praef 6.
9. Seneca, *Ep*, CII, 21.   1. *Idem*, XCII, 29–30.

The second characteristic which impresses a reader of Seneca is the importance of consistency, or steadfastness of character. Whoever lives a life according to nature must inevitably be consistent in everything. He is the same virtuous man in adversity and in prosperity, at home and in exile. His consistency is the source of his security.[2]

Although Epictetus and Marcus Aurelius differ widely in attitude and temperament, they emphasize the identical functions of virtue. In the writings of both we are impressed with the need to remember what things are in our power and what are not.[3] Reason discovers these things and at the same time leads us to exert ourselves only for the things in our power. As a result we find that one of the primary functions of virtue is the attainment of a new freedom. This freedom is obviously a freedom of soul, for political freedom is one of the things not in our power.[4]

The ethics of Stoicism is concentrated in the writings of Wordsworth published between 1807 and 1815. Only a chronological study of these writings can give us a sense of how completely Wordsworth's thought and work were influenced by the ancient Stoics. One of the chief reasons for the differences between Wordsworth's poems of 1800 and those of 1807 is the full emergence of a Stoic philosophy.

In the *Lyrical Ballads* of 1800 there is nothing comparable in idea to "The Character of the Happy Warrior," nothing to suggest that Wordsworth would one day write an ode on duty. In the 1800 volumes we find instead scorn for the Moralist, a man of "smooth-rubbed soul."[5] It is true that in 1800 Wordsworth was interested in the sources of man's staying powers, but he found these sources not at all in consistency and fortitude of character. In his adversity, Michael finds his staying power in the love he bears his son.

> There is a comfort in the strength of love;
> 'Twill make a thing endurable, which else
> Would overset the brain, or break the heart.[6]

Only a close chronological study may hope to mark the various stages of development which lie between the lines from "Michael" and these from *The White Doe of Rylstone*.

> Her soul doth in itself stand fast,
> Sustained by memory of the past

2. *Idem*, xcii, 3; cxx, 10–12; cxx, 18–9. *Dial*, ii ("De Constantia"), *passim*.

3. Epictetus, *Manual*, 1, Epictetus, *Discourses*, i, i, 2; i, xxii, 2; iii, xxiv, 1. Marcus Aurelius, *Meditations*, v, xv; vi, xxi; vi, xxx.

4. Epictetus, *Discourses*, i, xviii, 2; i, xix, 2; iv, i, *passim*. Marcus Aurelius, *Meditations*, vi, liii; viii, vi.

5. "A Poet's Epitaph," l. 29.   6. "Michael," ll. 448–50.

> And strength of Reason; held above
> The infirmities of mortal love.[7]

Since much of the poetry of 1807 was written in intervals during the composition of *The Prelude*, we might expect to find in *The Prelude* itself signs of Wordsworth's changing philosophy of ethics. To the comparisons already made between Wordsworth and the Stoics, *The Prelude* contributed a large share of examples. To a comparison of ethical philosophies it contributes little. The very scarcity of examples might be used to soften the criticism that finds "the authentic Wordsworth" missing from the philosophical sections of the revised version.[8] At the beginning and at the end, in the early and in the late versions, the only signs of a Stoic morality are those which Wordsworth's own temperament would naturally produce. His emphasis upon the stern and rigorous, upon man's powers of endurance, reflects the constitution of his own character.[9]

The poems published in 1807, which include some of Wordsworth's most Stoical writing, were composed mainly between 1802 and 1807. Of these the earliest are the "Sonnets Dedicated to Liberty." As we have already observed, the sonnets express a political ideal common to the Roman historian. In their Roman character the poems naturally suggest the Stoic philosophy which for so long constituted the religion of Rome. Just as virtue was the good of the philosopher, so it was also the good of the statesman. The civic virtue which preserves the state differs hardly at all from the virtue which preserves the individual. In celebrating the statesman who as an individual stands "*above* All consequences," Wordsworth expresses the most popular of all Stoic ideas.[1] It is the same when he writes of Milton in his character as statesman:

> Thy soul was like a Star, and dwelt apart;
> . . . and yet thy heart
> The lowliest duties on herself did lay.[2]

Thus Wordsworth selects for praise the embodiment of Stoical precepts: in his review of the duties that become the statesman, Cicero remarks, "ut recte praecipere videantur, qui monent, ut, quanto superiores simus, tanto nos geramus summissius."[3] But too much should not be made of the Stoic morality in Wordsworth's political sonnets. Had he read no more than the historians of Rome the sonnets would undoubtedly have been the same. In a study such as this

---

7. Lines 1623–6.   8. De Selincourt, *Prelude*, p. lxi.
9. *Prelude*, IV, 168–71; VIII, 215–56; X, 173–8; XIV, 244–7.
1. "The King of Sweden," ll. 10–11.
2. "Milton! thou shouldst be living at this hour," ll. 9–14.
3. Cicero, *De Officiis*, I, xxvi, 90.

they are significant only as they show Wordsworth prepared—as the Romans themselves were prepared—to accept the teaching of the Stoic philosophers.

A poem composed about the same time as the sonnets reveals a similar bias toward Stoic morality. In the poem "Resolution and Independence" the Stoic precept that warns against anxious anticipation of misfortunes receives its finest expression.[4] The "apt admonishment" is stated by the implication of the whole poem rather than by a bald imperative. The Stoic character of the admonishment becomes clear if it is contrasted with other philosophies that also counsel men to avoid worry over the future. In classic literature we think first of Horace, who, of course, often expresses Stoic ideas. But the poems in which he urges men to seize the present hour are based on an entirely different philosophy. We should enjoy the present and not think of the future because it is the lot of mortals inevitably to lose their present pleasures. We should not in our thoughts rush to meet the misfortunes that are bound to come.

> quid sit futurum cras, fuge quaerere et
> quem Fors dierum cumque dabit, lucro
>   appone nec dulces amores
>   sperne puer neque tu choreas,
>
> donec virenti canities abest
> morosa.[5]

The great difference between Horace and Wordsworth can be explained by reference to the Stoics. Stoicism recognizes the insecurity of wealth, of present pleasures, of all that is not within our power. But at the same time the Stoics deny that these things are good; virtue or—as Wordsworth sees it after his meeting with the leechgatherer—firmness of mind is a good that need never be lost.

In the "Ode to Duty," composed two years after "Resolution and Independence," Wordsworth expresses clearly and fully the ethical philosophy of the Stoics.[6] The poem is an invocation to duty, a prayer for constancy of mind and consistency of character. Wordsworth would now live obedient to the law of nature; in other words, he would become a Stoic.

The motto from Seneca, which Wordsworth chose for later editions of the poem, has been curiously ignored. All critics agree that the

---

4. For example of Stoics warning against fear for the future, see Seneca, *Ep*, XIII, *passim*; XCVIII, 5–6; XCVIII, 8. Epictetus, *Discourses*, II, xiii. Marcus Aurelius, *Meditations*, VII, vi.

5. Horace, *Odes*, I, ix.

6. For date of composition see E. H. Hartsell, *Times Literary Supplement*, May 30, 1935, and Nowell Smith, *Times Literary Supplement*, June 20, 1935.

poem is Stoical in thought but, except for Professor Beatty, no one considers that the Stoics themselves had much to do with the poem. Perhaps the thought that the philosophy of Stoicism was actually an influence upon the poem has been too obvious to be expressed. At any rate, Kant, Schiller, Boehme, and Vaughan have been proposed as possible influences.[7] A comparison has also been made between this poem and Horace's "Ode to Fortune." [8] The claims of Horace are certainly legitimate: Wordsworth says that his poem "is on the model of Gray's 'Ode to Adversity,' which is copied from Horace's 'Ode to Fortune.' "[9] But by this remark Wordsworth intended to confess no more than an indebtedness to the style and structure of Gray's hymn. The "Ode to Duty" and the "Hymn to Adversity" observe the same metric pattern and both are poems of invocation. Gray's poem is a fairly close "copy" of Horace's ode, although it is not by any means a translation.

In stating the central thought of Wordsworth's poem I have already referred to its Stoic nature, a nature explicitly described even in its title. But it may be worth calling attention to a few specific points of resemblance. Wordsworth recognizes two conceptions of duty: first, the exalted obedience to the laws of the universe, an obedience observed by the stars and by "the most ancient heavens"; second, an obedience to "humbler functions." Actually, these humbler functions are also laws of nature, for they are the laws of man's nature. Since reason is the law of man's nature, Wordsworth utters a truly Stoic prayer when he asks for "The confidence of reason."

According to the Stoics the man who fulfills his duty to nature, who lives in the light of reason, will attain an inviolable peace. To the poet who longs "for a repose that ever is the same" no philosophy could offer more than Stoicism. The Stoical way of life relieves a man of "chance-desires" and strengthens him to the point where his "hopes no more must change their name." "Nemo non cotidie et consilium mutat et votum . . . Magnam rem puta unum hominem agere. Praeter sapientem autem nemo unum agit, ceteri multiformes sumus."[1]

7. Rader, *op. cit.*, pp. 191–2; Stallknecht, *PMLA*, LII (1937), 230–7; Stallknecht, *Strange Seas of Thought*, pp. 128–30. Stallknecht argues strongly for the influence of Kant and Schiller upon this poem. He takes the Daniel quotation from Seneca for the title of his chapter ("How Poor a Thing is Man"), but ironically finds the Stoical elements coming not from Seneca but from Kant, "the modern Stoic" (*idem*, p. 206). Stallknecht does, however, quote Wordsworth's own statement that he " 'never read a word of German metaphysics' " (*idem*, p. 206, n. 8).
8. Thayer, *The Influence of Horace on the Chief English Poets of the Nineteenth Century*, pp. 61–2.
9. Isabella Fenwick note to "Ode to Duty" (*Prose Works*, III, 164).
1. Seneca, *Ep*, CXX, 21–2. For Stoic emphasis on tranquillity, see *idem*, XCII, 3; Seneca, *Dial*, III ("De Ira"), I, xxi, 4: "sola sublimis et excelsa virtus est, nec quicquam magnum est nisi quod simul placidum."

As the ode was originally published, the sixth stanza was devoted to the new liberty that the poet might hope to find in a life of duty. To the Stoics there was nothing paradoxical in thus anticipating a freedom based upon obedience to law.[2] Because such freedom is a good within our power, it is the only genuine freedom which the Stoics recognized. In the ode the poet looks forward to a wiser *second* will that shall choose submissiveness to the law of duty. In his willing choice will lie his freedom.[3] The idea of such a freedom is common to all Stoics. "Nihil cogor, nihil patior invitus nec servio deo sed assentior."[4] Although the philosophy of this stanza is perfectly organic to the new ethics, there is something unbecoming about it in the poem as a whole. The ode is an earnest prayer for the strict control of law; without a true knowledge of the nature of duty, a reader might find in the sixth stanza, which celebrates a greater freedom, something incongruous. At any rate, Wordsworth chose not to reprint the stanza.

It is here worth while to break the chronological study for the sake of Wordsworth's own criticism of the "Ode to Duty." In 1809, five years after the composition of his poem, Wordsworth still subscribes to the basic principles of Stoicism.[5] In his "Answer to the Letter of 'Mathetes,'" published in *The Friend,* Wordsworth explains the process by which a man may arrive at strict obedience to the law. The process is exactly that recommended by the Stoics. Duty begins, he says, with obedience to our own natures and, through that, to the universal laws of God and nature.[6] By the use of reason, and by that alone, a man discovers the laws of his own nature; he may begin with the contemplation of an external object but he must return to himself. Wordsworth's argument needs to be given in detail. An external object about which the feelings were once stimulated "may be re-

---

2. One is reminded of Cicero's remark in *Pro Cluentio* (LIII, 146), quoted in the previous chapter: "Legum denique idcirco omnes servi sumus, ut liberi esse possimus." See also Seneca, *De Beneficiis,* III, xx, 1–2; Seneca, *Dial,* VII ("De Vita Beata"), xv, 7; Epictetus, *Discourses,* I, xii, 2.

3. Wordsworth makes a clear prose statement of the same idea in his "Answer to the Letter of 'Mathetes'" (*Prose Works,* I, 326). Speaking of the time a man is forced to spend in "social duties," he says, "that time has been primarily surrendered through an act of obedience to a moral law established by himself, and therefore he moves them [social duties] also along the orbit of perfect liberty."

4. Seneca, *Dial,* I ("De Providentia"), v, 6. I have chosen the rejected sixth stanza for particular attention partly because it is the stanza upon which Professor Stallknecht bases his argument for the influence of Schiller. He thinks that the thought of this stanza qualifies Wordsworth's later "Stoicism" and that the stanza was removed on that account (*PMLA,* LII (1937), 230–7; *Strange Seas of Thought,* pp. 212–22).

5. The "Answer to the Letter of 'Mathetes'" (1809) proves that Miss Elizabeth Geen is mistaken in supposing an early repudiation of Stoicism: "by 1807 Wordsworth had rejected Stoicism as decisively as he had Godwinism in 1797." ("The Concept of Grace in Wordsworth's Poetry," *PMLA,* LVIII [1943], 701.)

6. *Prose Works,* I, 319.

called and contemplated . . . with . . . a sinking inward into ourselves from thought to thought."[7] Thus beginning with the senses a man may finally "endeavour to look through the system of his being, with the organ of reason, summoned to penetrate, as far as it has power, in discovery of the impelling forces and the governing laws."[8] Such a process of learning the laws of being is "long, difficult, winding, and oftentimes returning upon itself."[9]

Wordsworth has here described in much the same language the doctrine of the Stoics, as it appears in Seneca's "De Vita Beata."

Externa ratio quaerat sensibus inritata et capiens inde principia—nec enim habet aliud, unde conetur aut unde ad verum impetum capiat—, *at* in se revertatur. Nam mundus quoque cuncta conplectens rectorque universi deus in exteriora quidem tendit, sed tamen introsum undique in se redit. Idem nostra mens faciat; cum secuta sensus suos per illos se ad externa porrexerit, et illorum et sui potens sit.[1]

For the man who has attained such knowledge of self, Wordsworth and Seneca hold exactly similar prospects:

knowledge, efficacious for the production of virtue, is the ultimate end of all effort, the sole dispenser of complacency and repose . . . [Thought is superior to action] as proceeding and governing all action . . . and, secondly, as leading to elevation, the absolute possession of the individual mind, and to a consistency or harmony of the being within itself, which no outward agency can reach to disturb or to impair.[2]

Having commented upon the turning inward to laws of individual being, Seneca concludes:

Hoc modo una efficietur vis ac potestas concors sibi et ratio illa certa nascetur non dissidens nec haesitans in opinionibus conprensionibusque nec in persuasione, quae cum se disposuit et partibus suis consensit et, ut ita dicam, concinuit, summum bonum tetigit.[3]

In the letter to Mathetes, Wordsworth makes it perfectly clear that his prayer to duty, written five years previously, was a prayer for just such a Stoic conception of "The confidence of reason."

I may therefore assure my youthful correspondent, if he will endeavour to look into himself in the manner which I have exhorted him to do . . . to him in due time the prayer [will be] granted, which was uttered by

---

7. *Idem*, I, 319-20. Wordsworth's "Answer" contains greater emphasis upon the emotions, which are connected with sense perceptions, than a Stoic would allow. But his whole discussion is intended to "render plain the manner in which a process of intellectual improvements, the reverse of that which nature pursues, is by reason introduced" (*idem*, I, 318-19).

8. *Idem*, I, 320.   9. *Idem*, I, 325.

1. Seneca, *Dial*, VII ("De Vita Beata"), viii, 4.
2. *Prose Works*, I, 320, 321.
3. Seneca, *Dial*, VIII ("De Vita Beata"), viii, 5.

that living teacher ... when in his character of philosophical poet, having thought of morality as implying in its essence voluntary obedience, and producing the effect of order, he transfers in the transport of imagination, the law of moral to physical natures, and having contemplated, through the medium of that order, all modes of existence as subservient to one spirit, concludes his address to the power of duty in the following words:

> To humbler functions, awful power!
> I call thee: I myself commend
> Unto thy guidance from this hour;
> Oh, let my weakness have an end!
> Give unto me, made lowly wise,
> The spirit of self-sacrifice;
> The confidence of reason give,
> And in the light of truth thy bondman
>   let me live![4]

In my analysis of Wordsworth's criticism I have referred only to Seneca, but there is no reason why other Stoics could not have been drawn upon. Because of a similarity in language Seneca appeared to be the best choice, but in *De Finibus* Cato speaks of the same process working to the same end.[5] Epictetus many times urges the same endeavor,[6] and, by the very nature of the *Meditations* addressed to himself, Marcus Aurelius illustrates the endeavor in practice. Wordsworth's grasp of the philosophical concept of duty is, therefore, thoroughly *Stoical* in the classical sense of the word.

In an essay on Wordsworth, Professor Bush has raised some questions relevant to our study. He wonders whether Wordsworth's "faith in reason and discipline" is truly *classical*, whether Wordsworth "achieved a Sophoclean grasp of law and imaginative reason," or whether he reverted "to the mingled timidity and moralizing of the eighteenth-century classicist."[7] Professor Bush does not give an explicit answer, but he implies a fairly clear answer when he is forced to apologize for the "copy-book morality and conventional pietism" of Wordsworth's later poems.[8] If Wordsworth's Stoicism is as thoroughly classical as I believe it to be, the faults of his philosophy are also the faults of Roman Stoicism. In our praise of things classical, we are apt to identify the classical only with the Hellenic. But the Roman philosophy that began its training of the child with *sententiae* and progressed to the training of practical statesmen is as classical a

---

4. *Prose Works*, I, 326.
5. Cicero, *De Finibus*, III, vi, 21 to vii, 25; III, xxii, 75. See also Cicero, *Tusc Disp*, v, xxv, 70–2.
6. Epictetus, *Discourses*, II, xi; IV, vii, 6.
7. Bush, *Mythology and the Romantic Tradition in English Poetry*, p. 65.
8. Idem, p. 67.

philosophy as those of Plato or Sophocles. The answer to the questions raised by Professor Bush is that Wordsworth's philosophy is both classical *and* edifying.

The practical realistic nature of Wordsworth's Stoicism is apparent in another poem published in 1807. In "The Character of the Happy Warrior" Wordsworth describes an ideal Stoic hero.[9] Such a man is firm in his resolutions, capable of turning ill-fortune to good, eager to enter any conflict for the sake of honor, undismayed in adversity, and consistent with himself in prosperity. Since every aspect of this character has been fully described by Stoic philosophers, it is here possible to refer to only a few particular likenesses. Wordsworth's warrior is ready to encounter any peril for the sake of honor; "with sudden brightness, like a Man inspired," he enters conflict, and by enduring more becomes "more able to endure."

. . . ad omne pulchrum vir bonus sine ulla cunctatione procurret; stet illic licet carnifex, stet tortor atque ignis, perseverabit nec quid passurus, sed quid facturus sit, aspiciet.[1]

Quid mirum, si dure generosos spiritus deus temptat? Numquam virtutis molle documentum est. Verberat nos et lacerat fortuna: patiamur! Non est saevitia, certamen est, quod *quo* saepius adierimus, fortiores erimus.[2]

Actually the happy warrior suffers no ill, for everything that befalls him he turns to good.

> Who, doomed to go in company with Pain,
> And Fear, and Bloodshed, miserable train!
> Turns his necessity to glorious gain;
> In face of these doth exercise a power
> Which is our human nature's highest dower;
> Controls them and subdues, transmutes, bereaves
> Of their bad influence, and their good receives.[3]

A heaping up of parallel passages for this poem, or for others of 1807, shows only that Wordsworth has adopted in full the ethical teaching of the Stoics. Virtue is now for him the only good; it is attained by a life according to the laws of nature, laws which reason alone discovers; it is rewarded with peace, security, and constancy. Everything that is a man's own is controlled by his reason; anything not his own is outside him and cannot affect the permanence of his

---

9. For a full portrait of the virtuous man, see Seneca, *Ep*, CXX, 11–12.
1. Seneca, *Ep*, LXVI, 21. Cf. Seneca, *Ep*, LXXI, 28; Seneca, *NQ*, III, Praef, 12–13.
2. Seneca, *Dial*, I ("De Providentia"), iv, 12.
3. "The Character of the Happy Warrior," ll. 12–18. Cf. Seneca, *Ep*, LXXIV, 20; "Placeat homini, quicquid deo placuit; ob hoc ipsum se suaque miretur, quod non potest vinci, quod mala ipsa sub se tenet, quod ratione, qua valentius nihil est, casum doloremque et iniuriam subigit." Cf. also Seneca, *Ep*, XLV, 9.

inner tranquillity. In fact, the greater the adversity, the stronger and more consistent becomes the moral character. With such a faith Wordsworth can no longer regard the powers of external nature as the sole dependable sources for man's own happiness and power. Lord Clifford in the "Song at the Feast of Brougham Castle" was better for having known "The silence that is in the starry sky, The sleep that is among the lonely hills."[4] But Wordsworth no longer limits man's virtues to those fostered by the external forms of nature. Of Lord Clifford he adds, "Nor did he change; but kept in lofty place The wisdom which adversity had bred."[5]

In the same Stoical way Wordsworth recognizes the wisdom that he himself discovered in adversity. In "Elegiac Stanzas, Suggested by a Picture of Peele Castle," he speaks of adversity as "The deep distress" which "humanised" his soul.[6] By 1805 the word "humanise" meant to Wordsworth all that it meant to a Stoic. Whatever has been made human has been made rational, for reason is the ruling principle of man. In the light of reason man is prepared to face whatever happens. When reason prevails, "The light that never was, on sea or land" loses its power to deceive.

Between 1807 and 1815 Wordsworth continued to write poetry that expressed a Stoical morality. In these years he allowed the ethics of Stoicism for the first time to enter that prodigious "cathedral" of which *The Excursion* forms one part. Here Wordsworth made up for any slights done to ethics in *The Prelude;* in its second part the "philosophical poem, containing views of Man, Nature, and Society,"[7] is everywhere bulwarked with the ethics of Stoicism.

In the third book of *The Excursion* Wordsworth gives a general criticism of Stoic philosophy. The Solitary in his rôle of the despondent initiates the discussion: he protests that his is neither a pious nor an elevated mind,

> By philosophic discipline prepared
> For calm subjection to acknowledged law;
> Pleased to have been, contented not to be.[8]

He also finds no permanent satisfaction in the fanciful dreams of poetry that attempt to explain the nature of life. The Poet then takes up the question and suggests a more explicit condemnation of philosophy because, like poetry, it, too, frames a world and a life that can never be. He confidently attacks the Epicureans but questions whether or not the Stoics ought to be excepted—inasmuch as they worked for

---

4. Lines 163-4.   5. Lines 167-8.   6. Line 36.
7. Preface to *The Excursion*. (*The Poetical Works*, p. 754.)
8. *Excursion*, III, 267-9.

a "sterner quiet."[9] In the reply of the Solitary Wordsworth expresses the peculiar attractions of all philosophies and of Stoicism in particular. Philosophies are not to be condemned because the one noble end justifies the many various means. Any philosophy that sets as a goal the "life of peace, Stability without regret or fear" deserves the gratitude of all men. The description of such a philosophy gives us the whole aim of the later Stoics.

> The universal instinct of repose,
> The longing for confirmed tranquillity,
> Inward and outward . . .
> . . . the immortal Soul
> Consistent in self-rule; and heaven revealed
> To meditation in that quietness!—
> Such was their scheme.[1]

In his Stoic prayer to duty Wordsworth thought of a Stoic life as being well within the realm of possibility. In *The Excursion* we find doubts and hesitation. These are owing partly to the difficult imperatives of a philosophy as strict as Stoicism[2] and partly to the need for a "self-forgetting tenderness of heart."[3] Thus Wordsworth hits upon the ever-present obstacles to a life disciplined about the care of self. No defender of Stoicism would deny that it is an arduous philosophy, and common consent regularly protests against its lack of feeling.[4]

But Wordsworth does not forsake the chief ethical doctrines of Stoicism. In the passage which contains Daniel's translation from Seneca,[5] Wordsworth continues to write eloquently of the life of *Sapiens*. Despite the terrors and the failures of social revolution,

> . . . the wise
> Have still the keeping of their proper peace;
> Are guardians of their own tranquillity.
> They act, or they recede, observe, and feel;
> 'Knowing the heart of man is set to be
> The centre of this world, about the which
> Those revolutions of disturbances
> Still roll; where all the aspects of misery
> Predominate; whose strong effects are such
> As he must bear, being powerless to redress;
> And that unless above himself he can
> Erect himself, how poor a thing is man!'[6]

---

9. *Idem*, III, 354.
2. *Idem*, IV, 130, 1080–5; v, 500–04.
4. See Seneca, *De Clementia*, II, v, 2; Seneca, *Dial*, II ("De Constantia"), i, 1.
5. See above, pp. 44–5.
1. *Idem*, III, 397–406.
3. *Idem*, v, 576–9. See also IV, 351–8.
6. *Excursion*, IV, 320–31.

To win a "blest seclusion" and to feel "entire complacence" of will, man must still submit to the law of duty.[7] As Wordsworth's desire for permanence becomes more and more urgent, he comes to cherish duty mainly for its eternal nature. The laws are always with us, and by these laws "Duty exists," but nothing else—no possessions, opinions, passions.[8]

Again Wordsworth subscribes to the strict Stoic interpretation of duty as an obedience to the laws of nature. In obeying these laws man attains a self-consistency, a kind of self-permanence. The failures of men whose aims have been commendable have always been due to the fact that these "good" men were "The vacillating, inconsistent good."[9] The Wanderer, busy about the correction of despondency, holds out hopes for better days; he confidently looks forward to the time when "the instructed" shall learn "Their duties from all forms." The vision of such a future recalls the rejected sixth stanza of the "Ode to Duty."

> We shall be wise perforce; and, while inspired
> By choice, and conscious that the Will is free,
> Shall move unswerving, even as if impelled
> By strict necessity, along the path
> Of order and of good.[1]

Occasionally the life of reason shifts from that exalted vision of Seneca to the more practical and humbler *officia* of Cicero and Panaetius. The Pastor of *The Excursion* believes that "Reason, best reason" is "Still to be courted—never to be won." But for all of that he recommends a will subject to reason's law and holds out as a reward for such obedience the attainment of truths which reason alone could never reach.[2] The paradox here would delight a Stoic, for it is a paradox possible only to a highly integrated philosophy wherein logic and ethics differ only in function.

We come now to the last poem which expresses in any fullness a Stoical morality. *The White Doe of Rylstone* is particularly interesting because it shows Wordsworth at last the master of his new philosophy. In the "Ode to Duty" and "The Character of the Happy Warrior," there is hardly a line that could not be paralleled in the Roman philosophy. In *The White Doe* Wordsworth does more than merely restate the doctrines of the Stoics; he interprets, adds, and subtracts, and everywhere shows the sure hand of a trained critic.

7. *Idem*, IV, 1035–8.   8. *Idem*, IV, 66–73.
9. *Idem*, IV, 309.   1. *Idem*, IV, 1266–70.
2. *Idem*, V, 500–22. Cf. Cicero, *Tusc Disp*, IV, xv, 34: "virtus est adfectio animi constans . . . ex ea proficiscuntur honestae voluntates, sententiae, actiones omnisque recta ratio, quamquam ipsa virtus brevissime recta ratio dici potest."

Wordsworth manages his criticism of Stoic philosophy by the use of a subdued contrast between Francis, who is the true Stoic, and Emily, who becomes more than a Stoic.[3] Francis, significantly enough, is not the *Sapiens,* but his whole endeavor is to attain that rank. When adversity is certain, he urges his sister to hope nothing. In " 'the excess Of an unmerited distress; In that thy very strength must lie.' "[4] Her immediate and unflinching acceptance of doom, her continued strength and fortitude will be rewarded. She shall be,

> A Soul, by force of sorrows high,
> Uplifted to the purest sky
> Of undisturbed humanity![5]

Although Emily is not deluded by "The self-reliance of despair,"[6] she willingly submits to her duty.

> *Her duty is to stand and wait;*
> In resignation to abide
> The shock, AND FINALLY SECURE
> O'ER PAIN AND GRIEF A TRIUMPH PURE.[7]

Wordsworth does not describe Emily's long wait for triumph. Years pass unnoticed,[8] but it was only through a strict observance of duty that Emily at last won for herself strength to return to Rylstone and "put her fortitude to proof."[9] At this stage of her development Emily is a complete Stoic. By the "strength of Reason" she has brought everything that matters into her control.

> Behold her, like a virgin Queen,
> . . . . .
> . . . carrying inward a serene
> And perfect sway, through many a thought
> Of chance and change, that hath been brought
> To the subjection of a holy,
> Though stern and rigorous, melancholy![1]

Here is the high-water mark of Stoicism, and yet for Wordsworth it is not enough. Tenderness is wanting: Emily's triumph is not complete until its character has been modified by affections of tenderness, of gentle and unimpassioned love. With rare skill the white doe is again introduced. Throughout the poem she acts as a symbol and, in the end, as an agent of Emily's final victory. Through the awakened affections that she feels for the white doe, Emily's "stern and rigorous, melancholy" is changed:

3. Cf. Geen, *op. cit.,* pp. 702–04.   4. Lines 524–6.
5. Lines 585–7.   6. Line 1056.   7. Lines 1069–72.
8. Lines 1611–16.   9. Line 1620.   1. Lines 1590–7.

> ... a soul which now was blest
> With a soft spring-day of holy,
> Mild, and grateful, melancholy.[2]

Criticism of *The White Doe* varies between two extremes. Miss Geen believes that Wordsworth here plainly condemns the Stoic philosophy.[3] On the other hand, Professor Stallknecht finds *The White Doe* more "Stoical" than the 1807 "Ode to Duty."[4] As usual the truth probably lies in the mean. Stoicism enabled Emily to withstand the first shock and it eventually fortified her to the point where she could return to her desolated home. The "impenetrable" armour of Stoicism was at first a necessity. Once the blow had been withstood Emily could afford to admit the tender feelings and thus progress to a height beyond Stoicism.

The White Doe offers a good example of Wordsworth's use of philosophy. As an initiate he took up Stoicism with enthusiasm. He continued to reflect upon it long and carefully, as many passages in *The Excursion* will attest. In the end he did not repudiate Stoicism, but he used it as his own philosophy; with no regard to its logical construction as a systematic philosophy he enriched it where he most felt a need.

As we observed at the beginning of this study the ethics of Stoicism is an integral part of a whole philosophy. When it appears in the poetry of Wordsworth it appears in a context similar to the total philosophy of the ancients. After that context completed its slow change and became predominantly Christian, the ethics was necessarily modified. To understand this change it is necessary to speak briefly of Wordsworth's religion.

I agree with De Selincourt that Wordsworth probably never thought of himself as other than Christian.[5] He may possibly have felt some conscious opposition to Christian doctrine during that obscure period when he was under the influence of Godwin, but there all is uncertain. In the poetry of his most remarkable years, Wordsworth appears not to have intentionally contradicted Christian doctrine. True—much of that poetry draws its substance from religious experience not entirely acceptable to orthodox thought, but at the time when it was written Wordsworth gave no indication that he was aware of any heretical expression. If it is granted that Wordsworth always thought of himself as Christian, it is impossible to speak of his having suffered a religious conversion. Indeed, so long as he

---

2. Lines 1756–8. 3. Geen, *loc. cit.*
4. Stallknecht, *PMLA*, LII (1937), 237; Stallknecht, *Strange Seas of Thought*, pp. 221–2; p. 244: Wordsworth "retreated, as the years went by, further and further into his stoicism."
5. De Selincourt, *Prelude*, p. lvii.

thought himself always Christian, he could recognize no earlier and different faith which would need to be recanted. Although the cases are not exactly similar, it is worth remarking that Wordsworth made no vigorous repudiation of Hartley; in his later poetry Hartleian influences simply disappear.[6]

So it is with the Stoic influences upon Wordsworth. Wordsworth never repudiated the ethics of Stoicism; he made no determined attack upon the system for any apparent weakness within it, nor did he later find the system repugnant to Christian teachings. This should not be thought unnatural. After all, Christian ethics has absorbed many Stoical elements, and early Christians frequently regarded the writings of both Seneca and Marcus Aurelius as being peculiarly congenial to the gospel of Christ.[7] Seneca was even thought of as being himself a Christian and a saint.[8]

I am digressing somewhat in speaking of Wordsworth's religion, but I believe it is necessary to recognize that he did not become orthodox simply because he had tried Stoicism and found it wanting. At least, he himself nowhere suggests such a reason for turning to the Church. If a failure in Stoicism is not the cause for Wordsworth's growing dependence upon the Church, then the cause, whatever it may have been, does not here concern us. Perhaps, as his own religious experiences, mystical in nature, became rarer, he necessarily came to depend more upon orthodox revelation.

But, whatever the reason, Wordsworth's natural religion was replaced by a pure Christianity, and the ethics of Stoicism, which he once had embraced so wholeheartedly, was no longer perfectly fitted into an organic whole. Because the Christian religion offers a congenial context, Stoic ethics could in some cases be absorbed, but in some cases it was forced to disappear. For example, a Christian truly conscious of his sinning nature does not set up self-consistency as a goal of ethical behavior. Accordingly, the Christian Wordsworth ceases to talk of heaven's being revealed to men "consistent in self-rule."[9]

On the other hand, as a Christian Wordsworth continued to expound in part the ethics of the pagan philosophy. In his later poetry are occasional echoes of Stoicism that show a spirit somewhat detached and yet wholly sympathetic. The speech of Protesilaus in "Laodamia" urges a Stoical control of passion, a self-government of reason.[1] In this poem the ethics of Stoicism is no longer so clearly felt, but it is still respected as a noble philosophy of the pagan world.

6. Wordsworth here differs sharply from Coleridge. See Sir E. K. Chambers, *Samuel Taylor Coleridge* (Oxford, 1938), p. 139.
7. R. M. Wenley, *Stoicism and Its Influence* (New York, 1927), pp. 113 ff.
8. *The Cambridge Ancient History*, XI (Cambridge, 1936), 731.
9. Cf. *Excursion*, III, 403–05.   1. Lines 73–5, 139–42.

Had the ethical problem been as central to the poem as perhaps it should have been, Wordsworth would undoubtedly have found one right conclusion. Increasingly detached as he was, the fate of Laodamia varies with different editions of the poem.

The later political sonnets also show Wordsworth sympathetic to the teaching of Stoicism. In the sonnets he continues to celebrate the virtue of fortitude in a way which occasionally recalls stanzas of "The Happy Warrior." In spite of the submission of the Tyrolese to powers beyond their control, Wordsworth is confident that they still possess an inner freedom.

> We know that ye, beneath the stern control
> Of awful prudence, keep the unvanquished soul.[2]

So, too, when a noble leader suffers unmerited misfortune, he lives "to his inner self endeared."[3] These are plainly the sentiments of a Stoic philosophy. But for other martyrs to liberty Wordsworth finds a purely Christian consolation.

> . . . there lives
> A Judge, who, as man claims by merit, gives;
> To whose all-pondering mind a noble aim,
> Faithfully kept, is as a noble deed;
> In whose pure sight all virtue doth succeed.[4]

Actually, the virtue of fortitude remains the same; the difference is simply the difference between a philosophical and a religious context.

Thus, as Christianity came more and more to pervade the poetry of Wordsworth, Stoicism gradually faded away. Within a comparatively brief span of time, the philosophers of ancient Rome had to a large extent determined the character of Wordsworth's poetry. "Michael," "The Brothers," "Matthew," "Simon Lee" were poems written with a wonderful confidence in the power of "natural piety."[5] After that confidence was lost and the struggle for a new control had begun, Wordsworth found in Stoicism a source of new strength and vigor.

Modern critics have made much of the quietism and resignation of the Stoic philosophy. Mr. Eliot has described Stoicism as "the permanent substratum of a number of versions of cheering oneself up," and has sagely remarked that "A man does not join himself with the

---

2. "On the Final Submission of the Tyrolese," ll. 10-11.
3. "Call not the royal Swede unfortunate," l. 6.
4. "Brave Schill! by death delivered, take thy flight," ll. 10-14.
5. Cf. "My heart leaps up when I behold," ll. 7-9.
   "The Child is father of the Man;
   And I could wish my days to be
   Bound each to each by natural piety."

Universe so long as he has anything else to join himself with."[6] Such flippancies are sometimes as true as they are clever. Wordsworth was one who may well have needed to be cheered up, and by 1804 he certainly had little to join himself with. He had by then lost faith in the laws of civil society and he had not yet discovered the laws of Christian society. In that interim he turned Stoic, welcomed fortitude "And frequent sights of what is to be borne."[7] Such a form of cheering himself up was not an escape from a hostile world. Stoicism is a philosophy which demands and fosters a peculiar strength and force. In a brave attempt to meet these demands Wordsworth wrote the "Ode to Duty," *The Excursion, The White Doe of Rylstone.*

6. T. S. Eliot, *Shakespeare and the Stoicism of Seneca* (London, The Shakespeare Association, 1927), p. 9.
7. "Elegiac Stanzas, Suggested by a Picture of Peele Castle," ll. 57–8.

APPENDIX

WORDSWORTH's reading in the historical, political, and philosophical writing of Roman prose literature has been described in Chapters I and III. Evidence that he read other types of Roman prose is here presented.

Scriptores Rei Rusticae (Cato, Varro, Columella).

Wordsworth's Reference:
In a letter to Walter Savage Landor, January 21, 1824, Wordsworth writes as follows: "I am truly sensible of your kindness, as testified by the agreeable, and allow me to say valuable present of Books from your hand, but you will be mortified to hear as I was bitterly vexed, that some of them have been entirely spoilt by the salt water; and scarcely one has escaped injury. The two Volumes of de Re rustica in particular which I did not possess and had often wished to consult, are sorely damaged—the binding detached from the book, the leaves stained, and I fear rotted."[1]

Wordsworth's Copy[2]
Libri de re rustica. M. Catonis lib. I, M. Terentii Varronis lib. III. Per Petrum Victorium, ad veterum exemplarium fidem, suae integritati restituti . . . Parisiis, ex officina R. Stephani, 1543. 2 vols.

An anonymous article in *The North British Review* (1864) describes in detail a few of the annotations found in these two volumes and draws conclusions about Wordsworth's habits and taste in reading.[3]

The books are now in the Cornell University Library and are thus described in the catalogue of *The Wordsworth Collection:* "From Wordsworth's library and extensively marked and annotated by him."[4]

I am grateful to the Cornell University Library for allowing me to examine the two volumes of Wordsworth's *Scriptores Rei Rusticae*. Unhappily, a careful study of the annotations has led me to believe that the handwriting is not that of Wordsworth. I have compared the handwriting with autograph letters of Wordsworth (1824 and 1826), which are now in the Yale University Library,[5] and I have found persistent differences which cannot be accounted for by differences in external material.

Besides the differences in handwriting there are other reasons which make me doubt the authenticity of these notes:

1. *LY*, I, 133-4.
2. See *Rydal Mount*, Lot 361. (The abbreviated titles of the catalogue have been expanded and minor corrections in bibliography have been made.)
3. *The North British Review* (Edinburgh), XL (February–May, 1864), 84-6.
4. *The Wordsworth Collection, a Catalogue Compiled by Leslie Nathan Broughton* (Ithaca, Cornell University Library, 1931), p. 81.
5. William Wordsworth A.L.S. to James Montgomery, January 24, 1824; William Wordsworth A.L.S. to W. Strickland Cookson, December 26, 1826.

76 WORDSWORTH'S READING OF ROMAN PROSE

(1) The notes are in Latin, and Wordsworth disapproved of a modern use of Latin.[6]
(2) DeQuincey's remarks on Wordsworth's reading habits are in contradiction to these notes: "Wordsworth rarely, indeed, wrote on the margin of books; and, when he did, nothing could less illustrate his intellectual superiority. The comments were such as might have been made by anybody."[7]
(3) The notes show a special linguistic interest which is nowhere suggested in Wordsworth's writing.
(4) The annotations are extensive and they show a close reading; in his letters from about 1820 Wordsworth often refers to the weakness of his eyes and to his frequent dependence upon a reader and an amanuensis.[8]

For these reasons I have not used the volumes in my study of Wordsworth's reading of Latin prose. (See above, pp. 13–16)

Gaius Plinius Secundus

Wordsworth's References:

In a note to line 174 of "Laodamia" Wordsworth refers the reader to Pliny's *Natural History*, XVI, 44. According to the Isabella Fenwick note, the subject of "Laodamia" was first suggested to Wordsworth by Pliny's account of the trees growing and withering on the grave of Protesilaus.[9]

(*Naturalis Historia*, Jan and Mayhoff, eds. [Bibliotheca Teubneriana, 1870–97, 5 vols.], XVI, 44 [88]: "Sunt hodie ex adverso Iliensium urbis iuxta Hellespontum in Protesilai sepulchro arbores, quae omnibus ex eo aevis, cum in tantum adcrevere, ut Ilium aspiciant, inarescunt rursusque adolescunt.")

The motto for Wordsworth's "Vernal Ode" is drawn from Pliny's *Natural History*.

(*Naturalis Historia*, XI, 2[1]: "Sed turrigeros elephantorum miramur umeros taurorumque colla et truces in sublime iactus, tigrium rapinas, leonum iubas, *cum rerum natura nusquam magis quam in minimis tota sit.*")

Quintilian

Wordsworth's Reference:

In a letter to Charles James Fox, January 14, 1801, Wordsworth quotes the *Institutio Oratoria*, X, vii, 15: "The two Poems . . . were written with a view to shew that men who do not wear fine cloaths can feel deeply. 'Pectus enim est quod disertos facit, et vis mentis. Ideoque imperitis quoque, si modo sint aliquo affectu concitati, verba non desunt.'"[1]

6. See LY, I, 48.
7. *The Collected Writings of Thomas De Quincey*, II, 314.
8. See, for example, LY, I, 48, 68, 99, 109, 122, 134, 150, 206, 237.
9. *Prose Works*, III, 46.
1. EL, p. 262. The reference to Quintilian is given by De Selincourt.

APPENDIX 77

Wordsworth's Copies[2]
M. Fabii Quintiliani Institutionum oratoriarum libri duodecim. Novae huic editioni adiecit Fabianarum notarum spicilegium subcisivum Daniel Pareus. Accesserunt etiam Quintilianorum Declamationes . . . Londini, R. Whitakerus, 1641.

M. Fabii Quinctiliani De institutione oratoria libri duodecim . . . emendavit atque lectiones variantes adjecit Edmundus Gibson . . . Accedunt emendationum specimen et Tribunus Marianus, declamatio, nunc primum ex codice ms. edita . . . Oxoniae, impensis H. Cruttenden, 1693.

Gaius Plinius Caecilius Secundus

Wordsworth's References:
Descriptive Sketches (1793)
"Heedless how Pliny, musing here, survey'd
Old Roman boats and figures thro' the shade."[3]
In a letter to Coleridge, April 16, 1802, Wordsworth speaks of having read Pliny "many years ago." He praises Coleridge's extract from Pliny and approves his opinion of the *Letters*.[4] Coleridge's letter has apparently not been preserved.
"The Pillar of Trajan"
"And study Trajan as by Pliny seen."[5]

Wordsworth's Copy[6]
C. Plinii Caecilii Secundi Epistolarum Libri X & Panegyricus. Accedunt variantes lectiones. Lugd. Batavorum, Ex officina Elseviriorum, 1640.

2. *Rydal Mount*, Lots 389, 413.
3. *Descriptive Sketches* (1793), ll. 116–17, reprinted in *The Poetical Works of William Wordsworth*, E. De Selincourt, ed. (Oxford, 1940). For Pliny's descriptions of Como see *Epistulae*, I, 3; IX, 7.
4. *EL*, p. 287.
5. "The Pillar of Trajan," l. 28. For Pliny's correspondence with Trajan, see *Epistulae*, x, 1 ff.
6. *Rydal Mount*, Lot 410.

Index

Anderton, Basil, and Turnbull, T. E., *Catalogue of Books Concerning Greek and Latin Classics*, 15 n.
Annales patriotiques et littéraires, 8 n., 9 n.
Archives Parlementaires, 5 n., 8, 9 n.
Aristotle, *Politics*, 31
Arnold, E. Vernon, *Roman Stoicism*, 45 n., 46 n., 48 n., 54 n., 57 n.
Athenaeum, The, "Books from Wordsworth's Library," 13 n., 14 n.

Babeuf, Camillus Gracchus, 4, 39
Bacon, Francis, 44
Batho, Edith C., *The Later Wordsworth*, 20, 34 n.
Beatty, Arthur, ed. *Wordsworth: Representative Poems*, 12 n., 43, 44, 62
Beaupuy, Michel, 6–8, 11
Becker, Carl, *The Heavenly City of the Eighteenth-Century Philosophers*, 5 n., 6 n.; review by, 3 n.
Bimbenet, Eugène, *Histoire de la Ville d'Orléans*, 5 n.
Boehme, Jakob, 62
Boissier, Gaston, *Tacitus and Other Roman Studies*, 22 n.
Bolingbroke, Henry St. John, 44
Bradley, A. C., *Oxford Lectures on Poetry*, 43 n.
Brissot, J. P., 7–8, 10
Brissotins, 7
Broughton, L. N., *The Wordsworth Collection*, 13 n., 75 n.; *The Wordsworth Collection: A Supplement*, 13 n.
Bruun, Geoffrey, review by, 3 n.
Bury, J. B., *The Ancient Greek Historians*, 22 n.
Bush, Douglas, *Mythology and the Romantic Tradition in English Poetry*, 12 n., 65, 66
Bushnell, C. C., article by, 51 n.
Bussière, Georges and Émile Legouis, *Le Général Michel Beaupuy*, 6 n.

Caesar, Wordsworth's reading of, 14, 17
Cambridge Ancient History, The, 72 n.
Cambridge University, 1–2
Carra, Jean-Louis, 8
Casaubon, Isaac, 55 n.
Cassius Dio, 15

Cato, Marcus Porcius, 75
Catullus, 3
Cestre, Charles, *John Thelwall*, 10 n.
Chambers, Sir E. K., *Samuel Taylor Coleridge*, 72 n.
Cicero, philosophical thought of, chap. III, *passim*; political thought of, chap. II, *passim*; read and cited by French revolutionaries, 3; Wordsworth's reading of, 2, 13, 43; Wordsworth's use of, 26, 27 n.
Coleridge, Samuel Taylor, 10, 15, 44 n., 72 n., 77
Columella, 75
Cornell University Library, 75
Cooper, Lane, article by, 11–12
Courrier des départemens, 8 n.
Curtius Rufus, Quintus, 15

Daniel, Samuel, 44, 68
Darbishire, Helen, ed. *Wordsworth: Poems in Two Volumes*, 44 n.
De Quincey, Thomas, 1, 12, 16, 76
De Selincourt, Ernest, ed. *The Letters of William and Dorothy Wordsworth*, 1 n., 76 n.; ed. *The Prelude*, 5 n., 7 n., 8 n., 12 n., 14, 60, 71
Desmoulins, C., 5 n., 9 n.
Dicey, A. V., *The Statesmanship of Wordsworth*, 19, 21
Diogenes Laertius, life of Zeno, chap. III, *passim*; Wordsworth's reading of, 43
Dion, 6, 17, 40–42
Dove Cottage, The Official Catalogue of the Contents of, 13 n.

Eliot, T. S., *Shakespeare and the Stoicism of Seneca*, 73–74
Epictetus, philosophical thought of, chap. III, *passim*; Wordsworth's reading of, 43
Epicureans, 67
Epicurus, 45

Flamininus, 17, 27–28
Fletcher, F. T. H., *Montesquieu and English Politics*, 6 n.
Florus, political thought of, chap. II, *passim*; Wordsworth's reading of, 15, 17, 25 n., 30
Forster, John, *Walter Savage Landor*, 12 n., 13 n.

Fox, Charles James, 32, 76
Friend, The, 63

Geen, Elizabeth, article by, 63 n., 70 n., 71
Gibbon, Edward, 15
Girondists, 7–10
Godwin, William, 35 n.
Gorsas, Ant.-Jos., 8
Gray, Thomas, 62
Grimeston, Edward, 14–15
Grosart, Alexander B., ed. *The Prose Works of William Wordsworth,* 1 n., 25 n.
Gummere, Richard Mott, *Seneca and His Modern Message,* 44 n.

Harper, George McLean, 7
Hartley, David, 55, 72
Hartsell, E. H., article by, 61 n.
Harvard University, 13 n., 14 n., 15 n., 43 n.
Havens, Raymond Dexter, *The Mind of a Poet,* 7 n., 8 n., 12 n., 35, 51 n., 52 n.
Hawkshead School, 1
Hay, Camilla Hill, *Montaigne, lecteur et imitateur de Sénèque,* 44 n.
Herodian, 15
Horace, 3, 31–32, 61–62

Inge, William Ralph, *Studies of English Mystics,* 43 n., 48 n., 50, 52 n.

Kant, Immanuel, 62
Knight, William, ed. *The Poetical Works of William Wordsworth,* 1 n.

Lamb, Charles, 12–13
Landor, Walter Savage, 12–14, 75
Larsen, Jakob A. O., article by, 28 n.
Legouis, Émile, *The Early Life of William Wordsworth,* 6 n.; see Bussière
Levin, Lawrence Meyer, *The Political Doctrine of Montesquieu's Esprit des Lois,* 6 n.
Lienemann, K., *Die Belesenheit von William Wordsworth,* 1 n.
Livy, political thought of, chap. II, *passim;* read and cited by French revolutionaries, 3–4, 9; Wordsworth's reading of, 2, 14, 16–17, 28
Louvet de Couvrai, 9–10
Lowndes, W. T., *The Bibliographer's Manual,* 15 n.
Lucan, 51 n.

MacGillivray, J. R., article by, 4 n.; "Wordsworth and His Revolutionary Acquaintances," 5 n., 7 n.
Machiavelli, 14
Maigret, Louis, 15

Marcus Aurelius Antoninus, chap. III, *passim*
Maron, Eugène, *Histoire littéraire de la convention nationale,* 9 n.
Martin, A. D., *The Religion of Wordsworth,* 48 n.
Mathews, William, 19
Mill, John Stuart, 34
Montaigne, 44
Montesquieu, 3, 6, 10

Nepos, political thought of, chap. II, *passim;* Wordsworth's reading of, 15, 17
North, Christopher, 14–15
North British Review, The, 75

Palmer, Henrietta R., *List of English Editions and Translations of Greek and Latin Classics,* 15 n.
Panaetius, 69
Parker, Harold Talbot, *The Cult of Antiquity and the French Revolutionaries,* 3–4, 7 n., 8
Patton, C. H., *The Amherst Wordsworth Collection,* 13 n.
Phaedrus, *Fables,* 1
Plato, 31, 40, 45
Pliny, the Elder, 76
Pliny, the Younger, 77
Plutarch, political thought of, chap. II, *passim;* read and cited by French revolutionaries, 3–5, 10; Wordsworth's reading of, 12, 14, 16–17; Wordsworth's use of, 6, 17, 26, 27 n., 28, 30, 40–41
Pomponius Mela, 15
Polybius, political thought of, chap. II, *passim;* Wordsworth's reading of, 2, 14–17, 25 n., 29

Quintilian, 76–77

Rader, Melvin M., *Presiding Ideas in Wordsworth's Poetry,* 49 n., 52 n., 55 n., 62 n.
Roberts, W., article by, 13 n.
Robinson, Henry Crabb, 12, 13; *The Correspondence of Henry Crabb Robinson,* 13 n., 15 n.
Roland, Jeanne, *Mémoires,* 10
Rousseau, Jean Jacques, 4, 6–8, 10, 35
Rydal Mount Library Catalogue, The, 13–15, 16 n., 43 n., 44 n., 51 n., 75 n., 77 n.

St. John's College, 2
Sallust, political thought of, chap. II, *passim;* read and cited by French revolutionaries, 3, 9; Wordsworth's reading of, 15
Schiller, Johann Christoph Friedrich, 62

INDEX

Schmid, Wilhelm, and Otto Stählin, *Geschichte der Griechischen Literatur*, 28 n.
Seneca, philosophical thought of, chap. III, *passim;* Wordsworth's reading of, 44–45; Wordsworth's use of, 44–45, 61
Smith, Nowell, article by, 61 n.
Société des Amis de la Constitution, 7
Sonnenschein, E. A., article by, 43 n., 55 n.
Southey, Robert, 13
Spinoza, 49
Stallknecht, Newton P., article by, 62 n., 63 n.; *Strange Seas of Thought*, 43 n., 53 n., 62 n., 63 n., 71
Stoicism, chap. III, *passim;* philosophers of, 45; metaphysics of, 46–49; logic of, 53–55; ethics of, 56–59
Suetonius, 15
Swarthmore College Library, 1 n.

Tacitus, political thought of, chap. II, *passim;* read and cited by French revolutionaries, 3, 10; Wordsworth's reading of, 2, 12, 14, 16–17
Thayer, Mary Rebecca, *The Influence of Horace on the Chief English Poets of the Nineteenth Century*, 31 n., 62 n.
Thelwall, John, 10
Thevet, Andrew, 14
Times Literary Supplement (Notes on Sales), 13 n.
Turnbull, T. E., see Anderton

Valerius Maximus, 15
Varro, Marcus Terentius, 75
Vaughan, Henry, 62
Velleius Paterculus, 15
Vergil, 3, 31

Wenley, R. M., *Stoicism and Its Influence*, 72 n.
White, *An Examination of the Charge of Apostasy Against Wordsworth*, 11 n., 19
Wordsworth Christopher, *Memoirs of William Wordsworth*, 2 n., 4 n., 7 n.; *Scholae Academicae*, 2 n.
Wordsworth, Dorothy, 2, 8–9, 12, 17, 36
Wordsworth, William
    Philosophical thought of, chap. III, *passim,* esp. 50–53, 55–56, 59–74
    Political thought· of, chap. II, *passim*
    Reading in classics: At Hawkshead School, 1; at Cambridge, 2; influenced by residence in France, 3–9, 11; influenced by political writing in England, 10; habits in reading, 12, 15–16, 76; classical library, 12–15, 43, 75–77

    Views on classical history, 2, 5, 7, 11, 18, 21
    Writings: "Translation of part of the First Book of the Aeneid," 15 n.; "On a Celebrated Event in Ancient History," 27–29; "Ode to Apollo," 3 n.; "Apology for the French Revolution," 33 n., 37–38; "Avaunt all specious pliancy of mind," 25 n.; "Brave Schill! by death delivered," 73; "The Brothers," 73; "Song at the Feast of Brougham Castle," 67; "Call not the royal Swede unfortunate," 73; "The Convention of Cintra," chap. II, *passim,* esp. 19, 24–26, 28, 38, 42; "The Old Cumberland Beggar," 52; "The Death of a Starling—Catullus," 3 n.; *Descriptive Sketches*, 77; "Dion," 40–42; "Ode to Duty," 45, 52, 61–65, 69, 74; *An Evening Walk*, 3 n.; *The Excursion, passim,* esp. 25–27, 36, 44–45, 52–53, 67–69; "Gipsies," 52 n.; "Great Men have been among us," 27; "Hail, orient Conqueror of gloomy Night," 27; "The Horse," 3 n.; "Imitation of Juvenal," 15 n.; "It is not to be thought of that the Flood," 32 n.; "Laodamia," 72, 76; *Lyrical Ballads*, 59; "Answer to the Letter of 'Mathetes,'" 63–65; "Matthew," 73; *Memorials of a Tour in Italy*, 18, 21; "Michael," 32, 39 n., 59, 73; "Milton! thou shouldst be living," 60; "My heart leaps up when I behold," 73 n.; "O'erweening Statesmen have full long relied," 25 n.; "O Friend, I know not which way I must look," 27; "Orpheus and Eurydice," 3 n.; "Elegiac Stanzas suggested by a Picture of Peele Castle," 67, 74; "Personal Talk," 12 n.; "A Poet's Epitaph," 59; *The Prelude, passim,* esp. 6, 17, 25, 36, 49–51, 60; "Resolution and Independence," 61; "Written as a School Exercise at Hawkshead," 1; "Simon Lee," 73; "Sonnets Dedicated to Liberty," 60; "The King of Sweden," 60; "Lines Composed a Few Miles Above Tintern Abbey," 51; "The Pillar of Trajan," 77; "Two Addresses," 31 n., 36, 38–39; "On the Final Submission of the Tyrolese," 73; "Vernal Ode," 76; "The Character of the Happy Warrior," 59, 66, 69, 73; *The White Doe of Rylstone*, 59–60, 69–71, 74

Yale University Library, 75

Zeller, Eduard, "Die Philosophie der Griechen," 45 n., 46 n., 48 n.
Zeno, 45, 47